Down at the Local

Patricia Sumerling has been working for around fifteen years as a researcher into aspects of South Australian history, mainly in the heritage field. She has a particular interest in the heritage value and the social history of South Australian hotels.

Down at the Local

A HISTORY OF THE HOTELS OF KENSINGTON, NORWOOD & KENT TOWN

by
Patricia Sumerling

Kensington & Norwood Cultural Heritage Program

City of Norwood, Payneham & St Peters

Published by City of Norwood, Payneham & St Peters
in association with
Wakefield Press
Box 2266
Kent Town
South Australia 5071

First published 1998

Copyright © The Corporation of the City of Norwood, Payneham & St Peters, 1998

Patricia Sumerling asserts the moral right to be identified as the author of this work.

All rights reserved. This book is copyright. Apart from any fair dealings for the purposes of private study, research, criticism or review, as permitted under the Copyright Act, no part may be reproduced without written permission. Enquiries should be addressed to the publisher.

Project Manager Denise Schumann: Cultural Heritage Adviser
Designed by Liz Nicholson, design BITE, Adelaide
Typeset by Clinton Ellicott, MoBros, Adelaide
Printed and bound by Hyde Park Press, Adelaide

National Library of Australia
Cataloguing-in-Publication entry

Sumerling, Patricia, 1945– .
Down at the local: a history of hotels in Kensington, Norwood and Kent Town.

Includes index.
ISBN 1 86254 438 7.

1. Hotels – South Australia – Kensington – History.
2. Hotels – South Australia – Norwood – History.
3. Hotels – South Australia – Kent Town – History. I. Title.

647.949423101

Contents

Acknowledgements

This book was commissioned by the City of Norwood, Payneham & St Peters. The Corporation's Historian and Heritage Adviser Denise Schumann believed a social history of the hotels in the district was sadly lacking and made it possible for the publication to become a reality.

I am indebted to many people who are or once were associated with the district's hotels. Much enthusiasm for a history of the district's pubs was demonstrated by all the present publicans, who were not only keen to know more about their premises but to add their own stories as well. The former hoteliers that I interviewed from as far back as the Second World War proved that running a hotel is anything but dull. It was a pity that more hoteliers could not have been interviewed.

I am grateful to Bob Hoad who allowed me to utilise and quote from his revised edition of *Hotels and Publicans in South Australia.*

My friend Geoffrey Manning made available his newspaper database, and Alison Painter, Brian Samuels, Beth Brittle and Denise Schumann gave me much valuable advice concerning the manuscript.

Others whom I acknowledge for their support, information and loan of photographs are Chris and Con Angelopoulos, Dick Barratt, Brian Bingley, Chris, Matthew and Sue Binns, Colin Bond, Alan Brennan, Beth Brittle, Katherine Clancey, 'Clacka' (Gordon) Clark, Greg Crafter, Jimmy and Colleen Deane, Associate Professor Brian Dickey, Don Dunstan, Tony and George Franzon, Nick Grandioso, Jo Hastings, Wally (Wayne) Hodgens, Tony Jones of SA Brewing Co., Heinz Keimeier, Molly King, Hugh Lloyd, Macka MacKenzie, Rose Markovic, Barbara Mayfield, Ian Menzies, Deborah Mewitt, Phil Moore, Mortlock Library of South Australiana, May Murdoch, Dennis O'Donoghue, Rick Panizza, the late Des Pearce, David Pink, Genevieve and Peter Rumbelow, Rod and Jane Said, Adrian and Leon Saturno, Donald Scott, Kevin Shannon, Mark Smith, Joan Spangler, Dorothy Stentiford, Pat Thyer, Eddie Tunbridge, Arthur Wilson, Max and Githa Yeoman, Kensington & Norwood Civic Collection administered by Denise Schumann.

I save my last thanks for my very patient and understanding partner, Robert Martin, who had to listen endlessly to every yarn or morsel I found about a pub or its devotees and was then forced to read about it many times over.

Introduction

'There is nothing which has yet been contrived by man, by which so much happiness is produced as by a good tavern or inn.'
JAMES BOSWELL, *THE LIFE OF DR SAMUEL JOHNSON*

Down at the Local marks the culmination of a research project developed by the Kensington & Norwood Cultural Heritage Program. For the first time in South Australia a government body has acknowledged the importance of the hotel in society by commissioning a history devoted entirely to it.

The purpose of this book is to acknowledge the role of the hotel in society and to document its enduring legacy, its architecture. The hotels of Kensington, Norwood and Kent Town vary from the humble one-storey former Freemasons' in Wellington Street and the first Rising Sun Inn in Bridge Street to more flamboyant buildings such as the Norwood and Kent Town hotels. The mid-nineteenth century former Family Hotel on the corner of George and William streets in Norwood must rank as one of the most charming buildings in the entire council district, evoking the once village-like character of the neighbourhood.

Analysing the pattern of hotels in the Kensington, Norwood and Kent Town area will help explain why hotels came to be built in the first place and why several ceased to trade.

The section on the histories of the particular hotels includes illustrations and plans together with details of the owners, publicans, architects, clientele, and some of the events that have taken place in these pubs. I have attempted to convey the unique character of each hotel.

As this is a modest history, it has not been possible to write about every publican. However, Bob Hoad has graciously permitted his lists of publicans of the district's hotels to be included in this publication as an appendix. This is an updated listing from his forthcoming new edition of 'Hotels and Publicans in South Australia'.

Patricia Sumerling, Adelaide, 1998

Location of Hotels

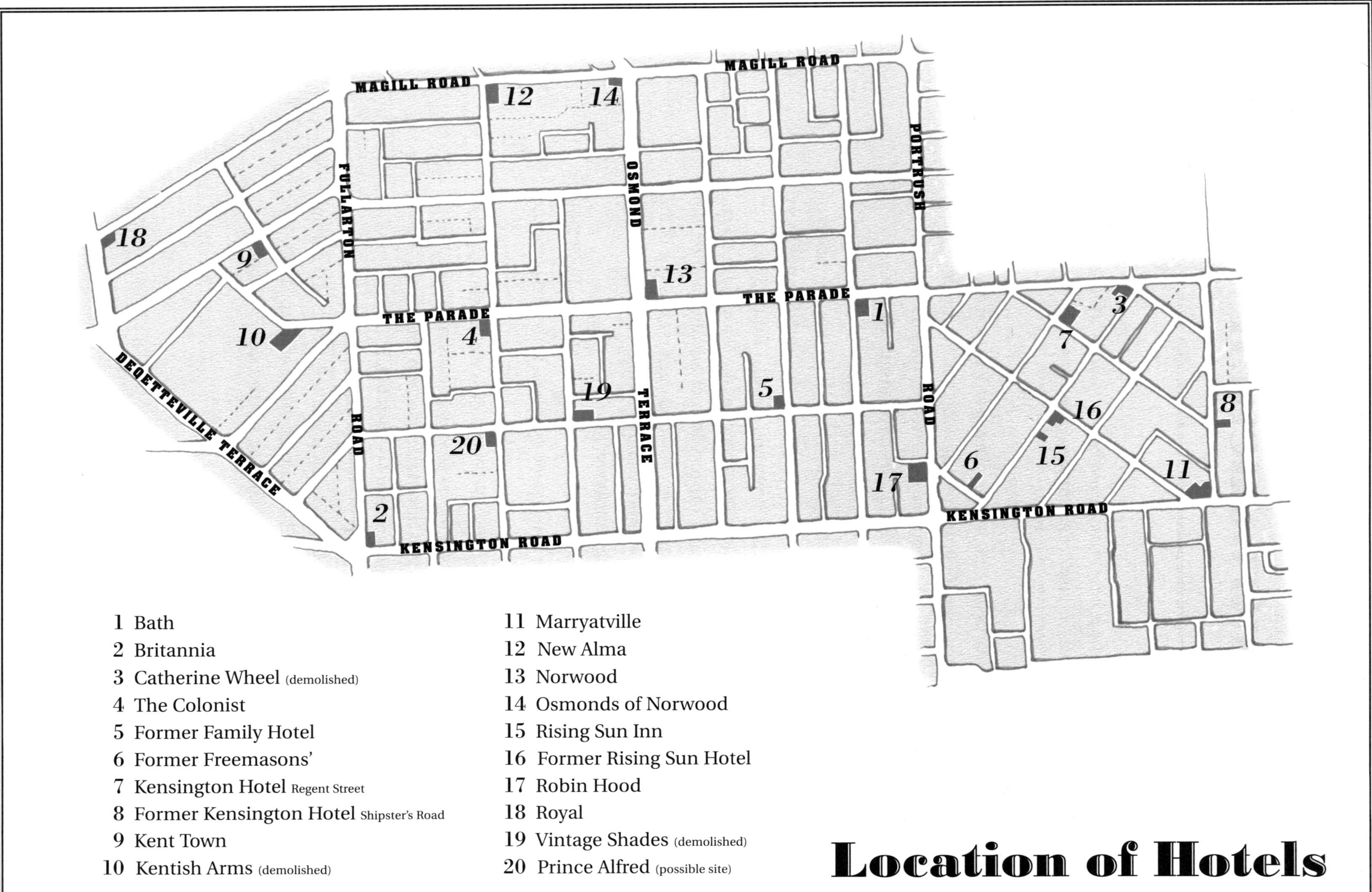

1 Bath
2 Britannia
3 Catherine Wheel (demolished)
4 The Colonist
5 Former Family Hotel
6 Former Freemasons'
7 Kensington Hotel Regent Street
8 Former Kensington Hotel Shipster's Road
9 Kent Town
10 Kentish Arms (demolished)
11 Marryatville
12 New Alma
13 Norwood
14 Osmonds of Norwood
15 Rising Sun Inn
16 Former Rising Sun Hotel
17 Robin Hood
18 Royal
19 Vintage Shades (demolished)
20 Prince Alfred (possible site)

PART ONE

UNCOVERING THE PAST

CHAPTER ONE

There's more to a pub than a drink

The main reason for the existence of a hotel has always been to sell liquor but there's more to a pub than a drink. Indeed, the social history of Australia's public houses is rich and diverse yet very little has been documented or published.

The pub was brought from Britain, along with many other British traditions. Devotees of the pub believe its role in British and Australian society was as important as that of the church. While parishioners would go along to their local vicar or priest to talk about their problems, for many other people their publican filled the same role.

"Rising Sun," Kensington.

WILLIAM BECK returns his sincere thanks to his friends and the public for all their past favours, and begs to announce his intention of running his conveyance daily, for the convenience of passenges and parcels, leaving the "Rising Sun," Kensington, at 9 a.m., and at 3 p.m., and will return from the "Red Lion," Rundle-street, at half-past 10 a.m., and at half-past 4 p.m.

Fares to or from 6d, and all parcels under 20 lbs. weight 3d.

He also further announces to his friends and the public, that it is his intention to sell Timber, Palings, Hay, and Corn out of his own yard.

Kensington, September 8th, 1849.

THE TRANSPORT SERVICE OFFERED BY THE RISING SUN INN. *SOUTH AUSTRALIAN REGISTER* 12 SEPTEMBER 1849

An early South Australian public house was a cosy, friendly home away from home and the name 'public house' was particularly apt as Mary Clancey of the Oriental Hotel on Osmond Terrace pointed out to her daughter-in-law. She believed there was never any privacy for the publican's family.[1]

The hotel was a publican's home but also a place where nearly anybody could share a drink in convivial company. However, the publican could refuse the custom of individuals they did not want on their premises. Sometimes publicans were forced to exercise this prerogative. Donald Scott, who took over the very rundown Kent Town Hotel in 1960, never hesitated to eject drunks, illegal 'bookies' and unruly customers from his hotel in an effort to improve the image of his pub.[2]

Publicans strove to give their hotels a personal touch and it was not unusual for clientele to abscond to another hotel if their regular publican left. This happened in 1967 when 'Macka' MacKenzie had a loyal band of his former clientele from the Edinburgh at Mitcham follow him to the Alma on Magill Road. When he moved on to the Rosewater Hotel eleven years later, a bus-load of his former Alma clientele turned up for the first cabaret that he organised there.

An incoming publican could deliberately alter the type of clientele coming into the hotel as did Max Yeoman at the Marryatville Hotel. He completely removed the draught wine pipes so that only pipes for draught beer remained. Similarly, at the Bath Hotel, Pat Thyer and her husband stopped serving flagon wine. This was done to deter a clientele known as 'wineys'.[3]

In British and Australian society, there is no place quite like a pub where you can simply have a drink, make yourself at home and linger on for hours until closing time without being moved on. In a pub people know they can meet friends, make new ones and be entertained.

Despite the ups and downs of the economy, the hotel industry has always survived difficult times. To stay financially solvent in more recent times, hotels have had to keep up with prevailing trends, be they poker machines, karaoke, rock bands, specialty food or choices of liquor. From the earliest days, hotels have often found a gimmick or a novel way in which to attract their clientele.

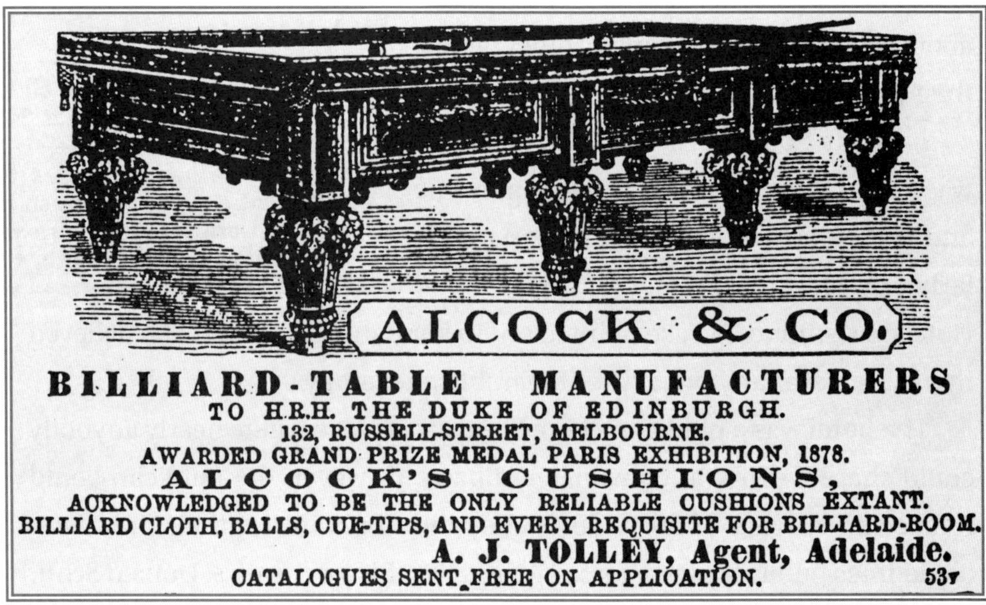

Advertisement for an Alcock & Co billiard table, of the type that was installed at The Colonist in 1881.
Licensed Victuallers' Gazette 8 March 1879

Horse and driver circa 1870. Kensington & Norwood Civic Collection

Hotels can be venues for many different activities besides the obvious one of drinking. Planned events organised by the publican or the customers have included a host of activities such as meetings of community organisations, balls, dances, concerts, fêtes, wedding banquets, sports meetings, dinners, lunches, festivals, sporting events, indoor games, chook raffles and lotteries.

Before the 1860s, pubs were rarely larger than about eight or nine rooms. Despite this, balls and dinners were accommodated without difficulty. According to local belief, one grand occasion took place in April 1859 at the Kent Town Hotel when many people attended a testimonial dinner for John McDouall Stuart, the explorer, who was setting out on one of his inland expeditions.

Men's societies and clubs met regularly at hotels until 1916 when the introduction of six o'clock closing made their evening meetings no longer possible. Local societies that met at hotels included the Ancient Order of Foresters from 1862 and the East Torrens Lodge, which met at the Bath Hotel from 1877.[4] The Kensington and Norwood Company of Volunteers met at the Robin Hood from the 1850s,[5] while in 1860[6] the Kent Town Rifle Corps conducted its meetings at the Kent Town Hotel. Facilities such as transport, informal letter boxes, job agencies and accommodation have been provided by publicans keen to maintain regular customers. In 1849 you could catch William Beck's daily cart from the Rising Sun in Kensington to the Red Lion in Rundle Street for a shilling for the round trip. Many of the Kensington and Norwood hotels in more recent times have had their own sporting clubs for cricket, football, golf and eight ball.

In the past legislation demanded that other events be held at the hotel: for example, coroner's inquests into sudden deaths and fires were conducted in hotels until 1908.

Often hotels have been the places of unplanned and spontaneous events, sometimes the result of people socialising together over a drink or two. Each hotel in Kensington and Norwood has its own swag of funny, tragic and absurd yarns concerning fires, murders, suicides, accidents and robberies, fights, parties and police raids.

RISING SUN HOTEL,
KENSINGTON.
J. P. DUNK, Proprietor.
begs to announce that he has succeeded Mr. W. H. Fairlie at the above well known and commodious suburban hotel, and trusts, by strict attention to business, and keeping only the best brands in liquors, to secure the same measure of support accorded to his predecessor.
Splendid Accommodation for Boarders.
Counter Luncheon daily from 11 a.m.

Advertisement for the 'counter lunch' at the Rising Sun Hotel. *Licensed Victuallers' Gazette* 1 January 1881

Pubs have almost always provided food. In the nineteenth century many pubs served what was known as an 'ordinary' every day at lunchtime. This midday meal usually included meat and vegetables. The landlord presided at the table with his wife carving and serving.[7] Landlord of the Oriental on Magill Road, A.W. Carlier, advertised his 'ordinary' in March 1883, also informing potential customers that 'a conveyance for Adelaide started from the door'.

Some hotels had weekly 'free and easys' which included food and entertainment in the form of singing, pianos and violins, usually beginning around 7 pm.

In the 1880s the counter meal was being advertised at the Rising Sun as a drawcard.[8] City hoteliers had begun to provide it at no charge and so customers expected a free lunch. Such generosity could and often did send a publican broke. Furthermore, this treat attracted the impoverished folk who would simply buy matches before helping themselves to the free nibbles. Not surprisingly in the early 1920s the counter meal dropped out of favour.[9]

Counter meals didn't really take off again for forty years. In 1961 at the Royal Hotel in Kent Town, Richard Barratt became one of the first publicans outside of Adelaide and the second in the state to offer a counter meal in the form of curry and rice or 'mutton and two veg'. In the first year of the new licensing hours in 1967, which extended opening hours to 10 pm, Macka Mackenzie started serving steak or ham and cheese sandwiches at the Alma Hotel.[10] At the Kent Town Hotel, Donald Scott began serving Gibbs' pies and pasties attracting a large lunchtime trade.

In the early days of the colony the local pub played a critical role in the social life of the village. Publicans often organised outdoor events in the grounds of their establishments. On Boxing Day in 1866, the landlord of the Robin Hood Hotel at Norwood held a fête in the grand English tradition to which about five hundred locals turned up for sack races, climbing the greasy pole, blindfold barrow races and quoits. Singing and dancing continued until midnight.[11]

The Norwood Hotel. Before it was rebuilt it was known as the Gold Diggers' Arms, circa 1870, Kensington & Norwood Civic Collection

Abraham Brooks, of the Norwood Hotel, organised a 'penny piece shooting' competition on 14 June 1850 in the parklands off West Terrace close to Emigration Square. For five pounds in prize money Thomas Skeuce and Henry Appleton shot at a hundred coins tossed into the air by Brooks over a two and a half hour period. Skeuce, the favourite, missed just one shot and won. A return match was held the following week back at the Norwood Hotel.[12]

In the late 1870s the Adelaide Hunt met several times at the Britannia Hotel in Norwood and went galloping across parklands and race course after a 'rabbit let loose'.[13]

The pubs of Kensington and Norwood were also popular venues for wedding receptions. Caroline Clarke, whose family lived near the Robin

Hood Hotel on Portrush Road, remembered watching through the garden fence as an assembly of a dozen brides and bridegrooms gathered at the hotel for a wedding breakfast with their friends.[14]

Edward Snell was twenty-nine years of age when he arrived in the new colony of South Australia. In his diary he wrote that at a wedding held on 19 April 1850, a bride and bridegroom were treated to rough music by the villagers in the evening, 'with a black fellow named Beck who keeps a public house acting as band master'. He was referring to William Beck, publican of the Rising Sun Inn at Kensington.[15]

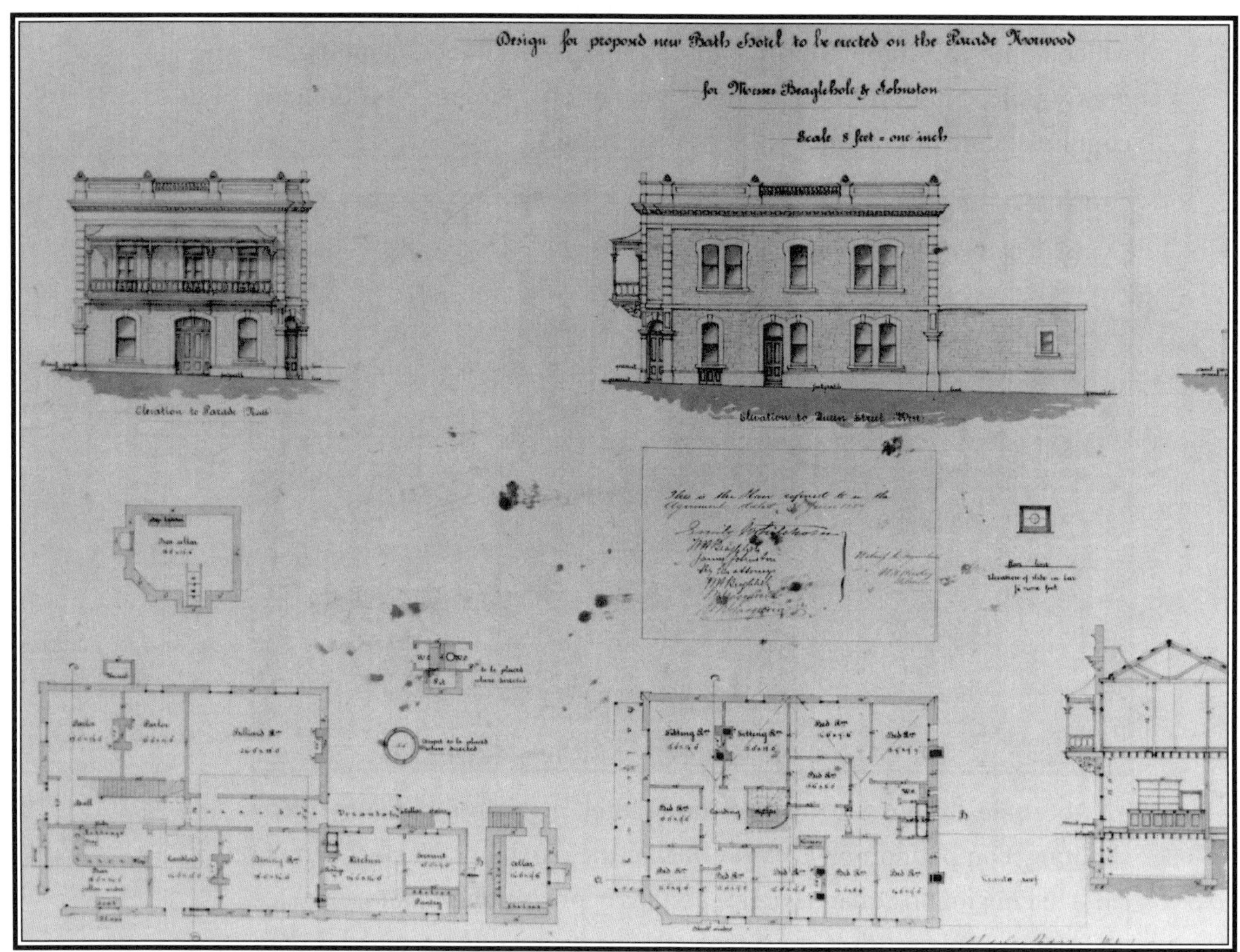

Plans for rebuilding the Bath Hotel, 1881. Morlock Library, Jackman & Gooden Collection

Hotels sometimes became galleries displaying unusual exhibits. In 1883 at the Rising Sun Hotel on the corner of High and Bridge streets, Kensington, an enormous mushroom looking like a Japanese umbrella, weighing two and a half pounds, and nearly three feet in circumference, was sent up from the Bush Inn at Willunga for viewing.[16] At the Bath Hotel, a fifty foot square choko vine was shown off in the 1930s. In the 1970s when Jimmy

Deane took over the Norwood Hotel and created the 'Sportsman Bar', he decorated it with large photographic portraits of sporting heroes. Many came to the hotel just to see the rogues' gallery.[17]

Although people went to hotels mainly to drink, comparatively few hoteliers in the past prided themselves on the quality of the liquor they sold. When Horace Yeoman, later joined by his son Max, managed the Marryatville Hotel from the late 1930s onwards, they took particular care to make sure that theirs was the best in the district. This was no mean feat, for in order to serve the best they had to thoroughly flush out the pipes after the pub closed and before it re-opened the next day.

Before 1909 the publican's pipes from his taps to the kegs in the cellar were made partly or wholly of lead. After this date lead pipes were banned with 'block tin pipes being the only ones to meet requirements'.[18] Although tin pipes were an improvement on the lead ones, even tin pipes, if not properly flushed, tainted the beer. From the 1950s onwards tin pipes were replaced with rubber or plastic. Now they are made entirely of plastic.

After the relaxation of liquor laws on 27 September 1967 women were gradually made more welcome in hotels, even in the 'inner sanctum', the front bar. Women started to play snooker and eight ball with the men and even set up their own teams.

Hotels took advantage of the extended opening hours by establishing social clubs. Events organised by these clubs often included whole families and they became remarkably popular.

Due to the later closing times, the idea that hotels were there to serve male and female clientele along with the notion that the quality of food and entertainment is as important as the provision of a place to drink, has seen the local pub change beyond recognition. Even though many hotels have kept their front bars, where diehard regulars can still feel at home and meet their cronies, most of the present-day Kensington, Norwood and Kent Town publicans agree that the appeal of the traditional male front bar is waning. People now expect that there is more to a pub than a drink.

CHAPTER TWO

A pattern of hotels

Adelaide is like the centre of a spider-web in that the earliest villages and townships were to be found on the main routes radiating from the centre. These included Magill, Port Adelaide, Gawler, Thebarton, Kensington, and Bowden which were all surveyed before 1840. Hotels appeared quickly in each.

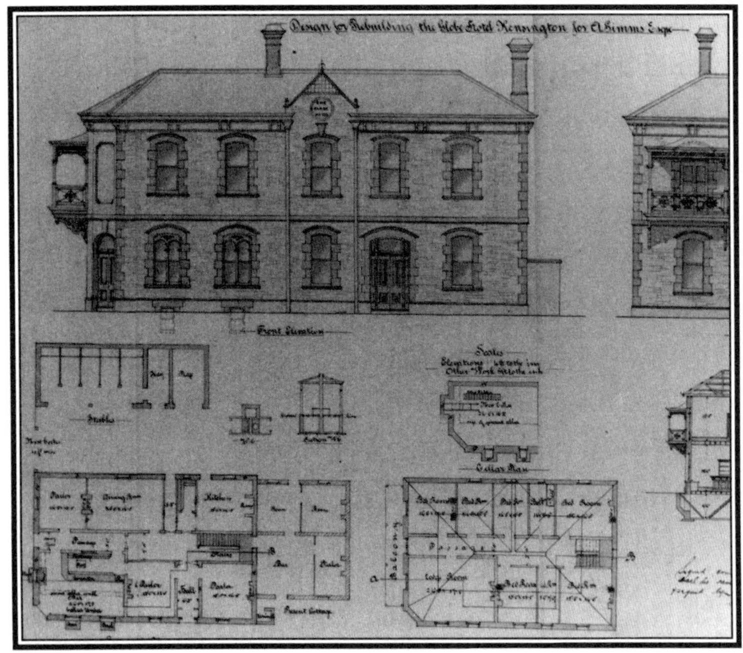

Plans for rebuilding the Globe Hotel, 1882. Mortlock Library of SA, Jackman & Gooden Collection

While hotels were nearly always found on main roads, some surviving hotels such as the Maylands, Earl of Leicester at Parkside, the first Rising Sun in Kensington, the Edinburgh at Mitcham, the Kensington, and the Wheatsheaf in Thebarton are now on streets that are no longer prominent.

The granting of publicans' licences across South Australia neatly mirrors the economic growth of the colony. In the early settlement period hotels grew rapidly in the mining districts of Kapunda, Burra and Yorke Peninsula during the early mineral discoveries. The 1870s saw the expansion of the railways along with the growth of towns in the mid-north such as Petersburg, Quorn and Terowie, and the Murray Riverlands followed in the 1890s. Hotels opened in each of these townships.

The early western suburbs of Adelaide were settled mainly by workers and local hotels were usually established with them in mind. Port Adelaide, Thebarton, Hindmarsh, Bowden, and Brompton were well supplied with public houses. The northern middle-class suburb of Prospect had considerably fewer public houses, as did most of the eastern suburbs – with the exception of Kensington and Norwood. While this district accommodated tradespeople and artisans, many workers lived in the small back streets.

The first hotel in Kensington, the Kensington Arms in Regent Street, was established shortly after settlement in June 1840. However, South Australia's first crippling depression meant this hotel ceased trading by the middle of 1842. Thirty-one other hotels throughout the colony suffered the same fate.[1]

VIEW OF THE PARADE LOOKING EAST 1910. KENSINGTON & NORWOOD CIVIC COLLECTION

The next hotel in Kensington, the Catherine Wheel, was established on the corner of Hill Street and The Parade and more than likely forced the Kensington Arms out of business. But this new hotel operated only briefly, until 1846. When the Catherine Wheel closed, the former Kensington Arms re-opened in March 1846, trading as the Robin Hood until 1849. After this it was rebuilt and its name was changed to the Globe.

Two years later Thomas Tasker applied for a new licence using the name of the Robin Hood. This hotel was located on Portrush Road and there is still a Robin Hood Hotel on the site.

So both the present Kensington Hotel and the present Robin Hood Hotel evolved from the same site.[2] The old Kensington Arms in Regent Street, Kensington, was demolished in 1849 and rebuilt as the Globe Hotel – a name it kept until 1958 when it was changed to the Kensington Hotel.

Two more hotels were subsequently established in Kensington: the Rising Sun Inn on Bridge Street in 1848 and the Freemasons' in Wellington Street in December 1850.

After the Kentish Arms lost its licence in the Local Option Polls of 1909, it became a private residence until its demolition in 1918. Kensington & Norwood Civic Collection

Land viewed as ideal for hotels was snatched up quickly during the subdivision of land allotments in Norwood in the late 1840s. The Norwood Hotel on The Parade was opened in March 1850 and was known as the Norwood Arms. This was followed a few months later by the Britannia Hotel on the corner of Kensington and Fullarton roads and, in April 1851, the Colonist Hotel on the Parade.

In 1855 the Alma, on the corner of Magill and Sydenham Roads, opened to serve a small local community and in the same year the new township of Kent Town had been surveyed. The Kentish Arms on The Parade West was established in the same year, followed by the Kent Town Hotel in 1856.

As the town of Kensington and Norwood grew, five more hotels began trading in the council district between 1856 and 1863. The first was the Bath Hotel at 232 The Parade in 1856. Then on Kensington Road in 1857 came the Marryatville Hotel, which later became the site of the first police station building and remained so until the new one along the road was built in 1908. Others established at the time included the Family Hotel on the corner of William and George streets in 1858 and the Vintage Shades at the corner of William and Elizabeth streets in 1859. In 1863 the Prince Alfred Hotel was established but it did not survive beyond that year, and has left no evidence of its whereabouts.

In 1863 Charles Hill, who went on to be master of the Adelaide School of Art and one of the early curators of the Art Gallery of South Australia, applied for a licence to open a hotel in Kensington to be called the Royal Standard. Described by the bench of magistrates as a 'highly respectable' man, Hill said his property was 'excellently situated' and that it 'would supply a desideratum which was greatly felt in the neighbourhood, namely proper accommodation for ladies and gentlemen travellers wanting to rest for an hour or two'.[3] Even though this may have been true nearby publicans objected to another hotel in their midst and managed to persuade 102 local residents to sign a petition against Hill's proposal. The petitioners said that the building intended for the hotel had 'no adequate accommodation for man or beast'. The licence was refused.

No more hotels were established in the town of Kensington and Norwood until the heady speculative years of the late 1870s and 1880s. This was a boom period for mining and agriculture, the staples of the colony's economy, and resulted in the development of new townships and suburbs served by new railway routes, roads and horse trams.

Three new hotels were built in the Kensington and Norwood district and most of the existing ones were rebuilt. The three new ones were the Royal Hotel in Kent Town in 1879, the Oriental Hotel at the corner of Osmond Terrace and Magill Road in 1880, and in 1881 the Kensington Hotel in Shipsters Road which is actually in the Burnside council district. In 1882 the new Rising Sun Hotel on the corner of High and Bridge streets in Kensington was built courtesy of Sir E.T. Smith, owner of the Kent Town Brewery. He transferred the licence from the Rising Sun Inn leaving this colonial building which dated from 1848 for posterity. The Norwood Hotel on The Parade was the last one in the district to be rebuilt, in 1884.

One of the key forces behind the redevelopment of the old hotels was the fact that by the 1870s the brewing companies were jostling for supremacy. One way to capture the trade was directly through hotel ownership and management. With the colonial government's Licensing Bench lobbying for stricter regulations about how a hotel should be designed and run, owners unable to update their premises either sold out to the brewers, who offered generous prices, or simply failed to renew their licences.

The upsurge in economic development throughout the 1870s and the early 1880s saw brewers renovate existing hotels or establish new ones that were usually more substantial and stylish than the privately owned ones.

In his unpublished history of the South Australian Brewing Company (1986) Michael Ogden says that of about eighty-two breweries established in South Australia from 1836 onwards, forty had gone out of production by 1888, leaving only twenty in the country and twenty-two in the metropolitan area.

In 1891 the establishment of the mighty South Australian Brewing Company was followed by amalgamations and mergers. This inevitably forced the weakest and smallest brewers out of business. By 1918 only five breweries were left in the metropolitan area and five in the country.[4] During this period most of the substantial hotels in Kensington and Norwood were owned or leased by the brewery companies.

Successful businessman, gentleman and mayor of Kensington and Norwood, Sir Edwin Smith, resided in the Victorian mansion known as The Acacias on Kensington Road, Marryatville. The Acacias now forms part of Loreto Convent.

Smith owned or leased seven local hotels from the 1860s. These hotels were the Alma, the present day Kensington, the Marryatville, the Norwood, the Robin Hood, the Rising Sun and the Colonist all of which he rebuilt or redeveloped. Apart from these, Smith had also bought many hotels or potential sites across South Australia when he was in partnership with Kent Town brewer Edward Logue who operated Logue's Brewery.

After Logue's death Smith negotiated a deal that meant five breweries, including the Kent Town and the West End Brewery, were incorporated in March, 1888, to form The South Australian Brewing, Malting and Wine and Spirit Company Limited. Before retiring Smith transferred all his personally owned hotel properties and eventually in 1891, the company became known as The South Australian Brewing Company.

The Licensing Bench played an important role in this era of redevelopment of South Australian hotels. It was able to restrict licences and to regulate hotel planning. The speculative building boom was peaking, and according to the Licensing Bench demand for new hotel licences had reached saturation point. The Bench required minimum standard

Sir E.T. Smith KCMG Mayor of Kensington and Norwood and owner of Kent Town Brewery, circa 1870. Kensington & Norwood Civic Collection

inclusions of room size and accommodation in hotel plans. It began to refuse licences in regions it considered already well supplied, namely the city and inner suburbs, and implemented a policy of rationalisation.[5]

In some suburbs potential hoteliers continually submitted applications to open a new hotel. They hoped either to wear down the members of the Bench or time their applications for when particular members were absent from a hearing. Licences for such hotels as the Oriental, the Waterfall Gully and the Maylands were only granted after several attempts.[6]

Reasons for refusals included the dense population in back streets where hotels were proposed, nearby publicans' objections to a potential threat to their trade or the Bench's decision that a new hotel was simply not required.

Some of the hotels which were planned for Norwood at the time and which did not actually go ahead were the Beulah, Knightsbridge, Junction, North Norwood, Burnside Terminus and Town Hall.[7]

Apart from these factors there were social reasons why hotels were being rationalised. The burgeoning temperance movement was beginning to make serious inroads into the liquor trade. Its members and advocates

Butcher shop opposite Kent Town Hotel, circa 1880s. Kensington & Norwood Civic Collection

gained key positions from which they could lobby for effective legislation. Out of this evolved the Local Option Polls. These polls were viewed with much foreboding by those in the liquor trade. Voters in districts (which were the same as those used for state elections) could either decide to reduce the number of hotels in their area, retain the existing number, or increase the number.

The Local Option Polls were a tool used by the temperance movement to further its long term aim of total prohibition. The Licensing Bench used the polls as an excuse to rid itself of its worst publicans and those 'houses which provided inferior service in poor quality premises', further reducing the number of privately owned hotels.

The brewers lost two hotels as a result of the 1909 Option Polls in the Kensington and Norwood district. These were the Family Hotel which was leased by the South Australian Brewing Company but was never rebuilt during the speculative boom and surprisingly, the impressive Rising Sun Hotel. Three privately owned hotels, the Kentish Arms on Norwood Parade West, the Vaughan's Kensington Hotel in Shipsters Road and the one-storey Vintage Shades in Sydenham Road all lost their licenses. One privately owned hotel that did survive the tussle was the substantial Kent Town Hotel. It was owned by a butcher, William Sims.

The pruning of hotels by a third of their number gave renewed vigour to those remaining in the industry. After the worst hotels were closed the standards in the existing ones rose. Business improved for the surviving hotels with customers looking for another place to drink after the loss of their 'local'. There have been no closures of hotels in Kensington, Norwood and Kent Town since 1909.

CHAPTER THREE

Hotel architecture

There are five distinct periods in South Australian hotel construction and to some extent they mirror the fluctuations of boom and bust that beset the colony and state.[1]

The first period dates from early settlement in 1836 to about the mid-1850s, when the gold rushes contributed to a time of rising prosperity throughout the colony.

The second period lasted from the 1850s until the mid-1870s and was followed by an era that saw a spectacular building boom. This was the third and finest period for hotel architecture and persisted until the end of the First World War.

The fourth period dates from the end of the war until about the mid-1950s, while the fifth extends from the mid-1950s until today. All the hotels in Kensington, Norwood and Kent Town were built before the First World War.

Prior to the 1850s, pubs were usually one-storey cottage-style buildings made of materials that were readily available such as pise, wood, brick or local stone with wooden shingle or slate roofs. They were built like private dwellings. What made them 'public houses' was the simple addition of one room set aside as the 'tap room' where liquor was served. The use of the word 'bar' came into more general use in about the 1880s. Food became part of what was on offer and accommodation was meant to be provided on request. After the 1850s this style of hotel continued to be built particularly in country areas.

It is easy to understand why publicans constructed such tiny hotels during this early period of settlement. The hotel licence itself was a major expense, costing a publican £100, and two of his friends £50 each as guarantors. Often the actual hotel structure was a secondary considera-tion to these monetary necessities.

Some of the earliest hotels were built in a temporary manner from cheap materials with neither 'doors nor windows, and they were in other respects wholly unfit for inns'. This did not go unnoticed by the magistrates of the Licensing Bench who, at a meeting in June 1851, discussed the existing legislation relating to such crude hotel premises.[2]

In December 1850 when William Powell applied for a licence for the Freemasons' in Wellington Street, Kensington, his premises were described as a 'low ill-constructed building' by members of the Licensing Bench.[3]

RISING SUN INN, BRIDGE STREET, KENSINGTON. DRAWING BY A.J. PEAKE. *KENSINGTON & NORWOOD SKETCHBOOK* 1976

The 1840 Kensington Arms was referred to as 'merely a mud hut' and was rebuilt in 1849 as a seven-room hotel called the Globe which is now known as the Kensington Hotel. Nothing of the earlier hotel survives.

A surviving example of an early hotel in the Kensington and Norwood district is the Rising Sun Inn, in Bridge Street dating from 1848. Its hipped roof forms can be clearly seen from the street. Another example is the former Freemasons' in Wellington Street, Kensington, established in 1850. This has been redeveloped over the years as a private residence.

During the 1850s, hotels started to look less like private dwellings and more like the buildings we recognise as hotels today. However, the interiors may still have been similar to those of the early period – by all appearances private dwellings, but with a bar and rooms set aside for accommodation.

The prosperity associated with the discovery of gold in eastern Australia saw the licensing of many new hotels and the rebuilding of earlier hotels in Kensington and Norwood. Many remained as single storey structures but were rebuilt using brick or stone. In this period there was little other adornment to the façades besides perhaps a parapet along the roof line or an ornamental pediment.

Hotels built in Norwood after the 1850s reflect the prosperity of South Australia when there was money available for more substantial buildings. The first Norwood Hotel hugged the corner of Osmond Terrace and The Parade. It was built as a one-storey, seven-room, solid stone and brick structure with sheds and stables, and had an annual rateable value in the 1850s of £100. For those days this was a large sum. Unfortunately nothing of this earlier hotel survives.

The former Family Hotel is perhaps the most charming building in the district. Located on the corner of George and William streets in Norwood it was designed and built by architect Thomas English in 1858. At the time he was beginning to make a name for himself as an architect and eventually he became one of South Australia's most sought after hotel designers. Many of his buildings have survived across the state.

In 1869 South Australia copied the British government's move of the same year towards greater control of the liquor trade by introducing special licensing magistrates in the licensing court.[4] Prior to these changes hearings were heard four times a year by magistrates or justices of the peace who made decisions that were not consistent from meeting to meeting.

After 1869 complex legal procedures meant magistrates attended to laws about hotel structure, room numbers, size and the type of building that a public house could operate in. Architectural plans had to be lodged at the same time as an application or for permission to rebuild. The mandatory structural requirements included regulations for minimum ceiling height and room size, as well as a minimum number of public rooms.

As regulations became more refined, so did the hotel buildings. Publicans of antiquated hotels who failed to comply with new regulations did not have their licences renewed and customers drifted to newer hotels nearby.

Regulations requiring the renovation of old hotels have brought about the closure of many pubs over time but the buildings have often survived. Many of these early hotels have been used as residences and offices and they are often better representations of what an earlier pub looked like than the ones that kept their licences and went on to modernise their interiors and remove the original fittings.

Very few hotels that were established or rebuilt during the 1870s and 1880s have survived with their original interiors. The two-storey former Rising Sun Hotel on the corner of Bridge and High streets, Kensington, has retained its original internal space and most of its fixtures and fittings. The bars and counters were removed when the hotel became a private residence after 1909.

Some pubs that were first licensed before the 1850s can claim to have been rebuilt at least twice, some three times, like the Kensington Hotel. Hotel design reached a peak in both flamboyance and elegance between the late 1870s and the early 1900s and many of South Australia's better-known hotels date from this period. Such buildings, usually of Italianate design with stucco ornamentation and later with shady verandahs in both cast-iron and wood, have contributed to the 'colonial' character of South Australia's architecture.

During the Victorian era, most of the early South Australian hotels were rebuilt. After this time, although the pace of building and rebuilding slowed down, the reigning styles, with slight variations to include Queen Anne or Edwardian finishes, persisted until the end of the First World War.

During the 1870s and until the end of the First World War, the hotel evolved into a fully fledged building type both internally and externally, much in the manner of a church, theatre, or private house with purpose-built spaces for different activities. At this time hotels had a number of public rooms and bedrooms. Minimum sizes for public rooms were specified by legislation. New hotels or rebuilt ones were nearly always two-storey and sometimes even three, like the Newmarket Hotel on the corner of West and North Terraces in the city. They often had chamfered entrances (these were specially designed for corner properties), balconies and verandahs, a certain amount of ornamentation on the façade, or carved ornamental stone.

The rebuilt hotels of the Kensington and Norwood district were variations on the style of the Royal Hotel, on North Terrace, Kent Town, which in

1878 was the first to be established as a two-storey hotel. As the need for large hotels became evident, prominent Adelaide architects competed to show off their styles. The Norwood Hotel and the Colonist demonstrate the district's more unusual styles. In 1884 the Norwood Hotel was completely rebuilt in red brick with flamboyant ornamentation.

In 1879 the Colonist had substantial additions and ornamentation but it remained a single-storey hotel until the twentieth century. There were additions and even new façades but the second storey was not added until 1912. The new façade then was designed to blend in with the one that had been added to the lower storey in 1879.

Old Colonist hotel before the upper storey was added, circa 1911. Photo courtesy of Genevieve Rumbelow

In the 1920s further additions were made along the Sydenham Road frontage together with a verandah that was later removed in 1954. Today the Colonist has an unusual asymmetrical design, and is the only example of a hotel in the district that has evolved stage by stage from the early 1850s to its present form whilst retaining some feature of each stage.

One of the biggest changes to the interiors of pubs was caused by six o'clock closing, which was introduced in 1916 and lasted until 1967. Early closing and the custom of the 'shout', where each man in a group bought a round of drinks before six o'clock, led to rowdy and raucous behaviour. The reputation of the front bar spread far and wide.

Old Colonist hotel with its verandah and balcony before the late 1920s.
Photo courtesy of Genevieve Rumbelow

To cope with this new environment of crowded front bars awash with spilt beer, many publicans enlarged their front bars by knocking several rooms into one. Tiles and terrazzo were laid on the walls and floors of the new bar and publicans added cement or terrazzo gutters at the base of the bars. These 'spit and sawdust' features are still found in many hotels throughout South Australia. Osmonds, on the corner of Osmond Terrace and Magill Road, has kept its guttering at the base of its front bar counter but otherwise in the Kensington and Norwood district, few features associated with six o'clock closing have survived.

CHAPTER FOUR

Changing licensing laws

The production, sale and control of liquor was vital to the life of the colony. One of the first half-dozen government bills passed in South Australia, in February 1837, was for the regulation of sales of liquor and the promotion of good order in public houses.[1]

By December 1838 this first licensing act had been replaced but elements such as the 'promotion of good order in public houses' were retained. In March 1846 William Beck, innkeeper of the Robin Hood at Kensington, pleaded guilty to the charge of 'having on the occasion of his opening entertainment admitted loose and bad characters about his house' and he was fined two guineas.[2]

Between 1838 and 1869 applications for licences were vetted by members of the judiciary such as magistrates or justices of the peace and usually residents were encouraged to 'attend and vote and act'.[3] Act they certainly did, for they called upon witnesses to give information about the moral character of applicants.

In the case of William Akehurst, who applied for a licence at the Robin Hood Hotel in 1849, police inspector Alexander Tolmer gave damning evidence that Akehurst was a former convict from Van Diemen's Land. On the strength of this evidence, even though the applicant had been a free man in South Australia for many years, the justices were adamant in refusing a licence 'to this class of person', and asked 'whether we are to have convicts or not for publicans?'[4]

The Licensing Act of 1869 provided for the setting up of Licensing Benches consisting of nine justices of the peace with three forming a quorum.[5] The Bench decided who was eligible for a licence, whether licences would be renewed or transferred, and decided who would lose their licences.

Once accepted by the Bench as being of good moral character and worthy of a licence, the potential publican then needed to pay for the licence, and it was an expensive business. First there was the £25 for the general publican's licence, together with three recognisances. One recognisance of £100 had to be provided by the applicant himself and two of £50 as surety.[6] Other than the general publican's licence there were two other licences to purchase. One was a 'wine, ale, beer and other malt liquors only' licence. The other was a storekeeper's licence.

Until the 1880s legislation demanded that hotels have a light burning outside from dusk until dawn. This provided many a headache for publicans, who explained to authorities that the lamps would blow out on stormy nights. More often than not they 'forgot' to light them. Such excuses held no water and it was not unusual for several hapless publicans at a time to appear in court. As well, the tiresome chore was not without its dangers. William Dumbleton, the first landlord of the Newmarket Hotel in the city, fell off his ladder and broke his neck as he drunkenly tried to light his lamp. There were other dangers too. In 1858 the wisdom of demanding lights on public houses facing seafronts was debated in parliament after a ship had sailed into five fathoms of water when the captain had mistaken a pub's light in Glenelg for a lighthouse.[7]

The liquor industry has always been heavily regulated and at times publicans have had to allow their hotels to be used for unusual purposes. From 1839 until 1908 hoteliers had to receive corpses for coroners' inquests. The first amendment to this act was in 1869, after which a publican was still required to receive a corpse unless there was a police station with cells within one mile of the hotel. In 1880 this was amended to two miles.

In 1908 the regulation swung a little further in the publican's favour when he could then refuse to accommodate a corpse if it was decomposed, or if the person had died from an infectious disease.

Many of the hotels in Kensington, Norwood and Kent Town have been the venue for coroners' inquests. In 1851 the Robin Hood Hotel was the venue for the investigation of a suspected infanticide case involving the new born infant of Jane Cardion.[8] An inquest was held at the Britannia Hotel in March 1856 after soap and candle maker Thomas Spain hanged himself at Rundle Street, Kent Town. It was found that Spain committed suicide because he owed a large sum of money after his workshop had been flooded and his candlemaking business ruined.[9]

At the Alma an inquest was held in June 1881 into the case of Amelia Mickley who died from the effects of drinking.[10] In November 1893,

Louis A. Rothenberg, publican of the Rising Sun Hotel, hanged himself in the pub after his racehorse was killed during a Tattersalls' race.[11] In January 1907 an inquest was held at the Oriental Hotel after William Gadkear and his wife were accidentally drowned in Cox's pughole on the corner of Stephen Street and Osmond Terrace.[12]

Hotels were often the largest buildings in a village or district until town halls or institutes were built, so they were used as election polling booths before 1857. The community hotly debated whether voters who took advantage of free beer, paid for by contesting parliamentarians, were influenced by such generosity.

Some unfortunate publicans were left unpaid bills by forgetful candidates. In 1856 during the nominations for East Torrens, the Globe's publican, Ed Shakel, took the contestant J.B. Hughes to court for non-payment of his excessive entertainment bill run up on election day in the previous September. The publican had been asked to provide beer for the voters and feed the musicians of a band that had been hired to entertain them. Shakel had welcomed the extra trade but it ended badly when the electoral candidate Hughes failed to reimburse him.

In the same election Mr Beddies of the Maid and Magpie Hotel at Stepney also found himself out of pocket thanks to Hughes, so the two publicans took him to court. Only Shakel was reimbursed, the judge deciding that he 'did not see anything in the case to warrant the conclusion that corrupt practices were resorted to. The employment of a band would not necessarily corrupt voters and he would give judgement for the amount claimed'. Beddies was not reimbursed because he was seen as being a party to bribery at an election. The judge then reminded everyone that 'it would shock all common sense, if the law would enable conspirators to recover between themselves money expended for the purpose of procuring a breach of the law. In all such cases the parties must rely on the principle of "honour among thieves", as the law could not uphold a breach of the law'. A year later, providing free beer at hotels during elections ceased to be a problem because polling booths were moved to places of less temptation.[13]

In 1839 hotels were open until ten at night and this was the case until 1855 when the time changed to eleven. This was extended for an extra hour on special occasions such as balls if written permission was gained from two justices of the peace. This was done by the publican at the Robin Hood who organised a fête around his hotel on Boxing Day in 1866. It started at noon and finished promptly at midnight.

From the late 1830s till the 1900s bona fide travellers could be served liquor outside official closing times. This legislation was occasionally tested by locals pretending to be travellers. In 1880 Michael Ryan of the Britannia Hotel was charged with supplying beer to two customers who insisted they were bona fide travellers.[14]

Until 1910 a bona fide traveller was defined as one who had travelled more than seven miles during the day. As motor cars became more common, a bona fide traveller had to have travelled at least fifty miles and be assigned a bed which he had to sign for. Many cases testing the validity of a bona fide traveller were brought before the courts during the years when the hotels closed at six o'clock.

Norwood police outside the station on Osmond Terrace in 1882.
Kensington & Norwood Civic Collection

The legislation enforcing six o'clock closing operated between 1916 and 1967. It made extra work for the police, who had to mount regular patrols to make inspections of licensed premises. As for the publicans who chose to ignore the prescribed closing times, they had to find a way of escaping the long arm of the law.

Indeed, part of the entertainment in a hotel during this time was the thrill of evading after-hours police raids. The police in Norwood generally patrolled their areas at regular intervals and were sometimes very strict. At other times they turned a blind eye. Police activities in the Norwood hotels cannot be properly studied as records for the Norwood district survive for only about three years in the 1920s. But in these skimpy records a few cases relating to abuse of the liquor laws were noted.

On 14 October 1920 at the Oriental on Osmond Terrace at about 7.30 pm, James Webber, husband of the licensee, was found to have had the side window of the bar open. Drinks were still on the servery and four men were in the passage. It is not recorded how far this case went but a report was forwarded by the constables on duty to the inspector in Norwood.[15]

This incident at the Oriental Hotel occurred during a sudden increase in surveillance of hotels from August 1920 until at least February 1921. Police organised two and sometimes three police patrols of two men, six nights a week and throughout Sunday. One disgruntled wife in the Payneham area, whose husband was always at the pub on Sundays when the hotels were supposed to be shut, dobbed in those hotels she knew in the Payneham, Hampstead and Modbury districts that did their best trade on Sundays.[16]

The records indicate that at this time the Bath and the Colonist were given special attention. In February 1921 the Colonist was visited three times, while on Saturday 2 October 1920, the Bath was visited five times between 6.15 and 10.45 pm.[17] However, these two pubs were never caught out in this period. This suggests either that they really were closed for business or that their lookouts, known as 'nit-keepers' and 'cockatoos', were exceptionally skilled.

At about 8.30 pm on 21 December 1920 the Norwood police paid an unscheduled call to the Globe in Kensington, which was meant to be under the watchful eye of the Marryatville Police, and caught the hotel trading after hours. This visit by the Norwood Police to the Globe was the only one they ever made in this period.

In March 1934 the licensee of the Colonist was charged with supplying liquor after hours. When the police visited the premises they found the door locked. On entering they saw the publican's wife running to the dining room with a tray of used glasses. As the police dashed after her, two men rushed past out the front door locking it behind them and so making it difficult for the police to catch them before they disappeared into the night. The licensee refused to explain who had drunk the liquor in the four glasses. In court the licensee said that one of those who ran away was his son and the other was the barman. The licensee's son said he ran away because he didn't know whether he was allowed to have a drink. The special magistrate believed the defence and held that the son had slept at the hotel immediately preceding the day of the alleged offence and so the case was dismissed.[18]

By the mid-1950s all Australian states except South Australia and Victoria had abolished six o'clock closing. It was a decade later before Victoria and South Australia extended trading hours and so ended fifty years of prohibitive trading.

Another of the dubious activities publicans engaged in was tampering with the quality of their wines, beers and spirits by watering them down or adding other concoctions. But this could be difficult to prove. In 1880 Mary Pearce, the publican at Crampton's Family Hotel on the corner of George and William streets was taken to court for adulterating the brandy which was served at the hotel.[19] She was acquitted though one wonders how the allegations affected her trade.

It is said that Australians will bet on two flies climbing up a wall. Not surprisingly, gambling in many illegal forms in hotels has a long history.

Former publican of the Norwood Hotel, Jimmy Deane, admits to having an SP bookie at the hotel in the mid-1970s. At the Bath Hotel it was well-known that the bookie was the hotel's own barmaid. The Oriental Hotel, known for its elegant mirrored premises under the management of Mary Clancey, had its own bookie who was never caught despite frequent attempts to trap him. After retiring he moved into the hotel and lived there permanently.

Some publicans had to allow bookies on their premises because, as Dick Barratt of the Royal Hotel said, 'if you didn't, customers would go to a hotel where there was one'. But not all of them welcomed bookies or other gambling. Max Yeoman, publican of the Marryatville Hotel after the Second World War, never tolerated a bookie.

Donald Scott took over the Kent Town Hotel in the 1960s when it was run-down and had a poor reputation, and he was determined to build up the business. He could not afford to lose his licence through illegal gambling. On two different occasions he discovered bookies operating covertly and banished them but not before one of them almost cost him his licence. Illegal gambling was considered such a serious offence during this time that a publican with only one conviction against him for allowing betting on his premises could lose his licence altogether.

As is often the case with prohibitions, the ban on gambling caused illegal gambling to flourish. No doubt it would still persist in hotels had legislation not been passed to allow gambling to be practised in a well-regulated and open manner.

CHAPTER FIVE

No place for a woman

It is interesting to note that the lives of women publicans and barmaids in South Australia have never been closely studied and it goes without saying that the district of Kensington and Norwood had its fair share of notable women involved in the hotel industry.

Two hotels in the district had female publicans who became local institutions because of their long careers in the trade. Anna Davis managed the Robin Hood Hotel for forty-three years from 1914 until 1957, and Mary Clancey of the Oriental Hotel on the corner of Osmond Terrace and Magill Road was publican from 1925 until 1971. Each carried on their husband's licences after their partners died. Mary and Anna's careers as publicans at one hotel are longer than for any male publican in the district. Two other women publicans who managed their hotels with their husbands for long periods in Norwood were Mrs Albertina Tasker of the Norwood Hotel and Mrs Euphemia Moore of the Colonist.[1]

The management of public houses was usually undertaken by men, but an indication of numbers of female publicans was given in 1908 when it was quoted in parliament that 'of over 700 hotels in the State more than one-fourth are in the possession of the fair sex'.[2]

For most male publicans their wives assumed the status of invisible business partners. This came about through the practice of granting hotel licences in one name. Couples found there was an advantage in putting the licences in only the husband's or wife's name. If a licensee incurred three convictions within a given period and thus was liable to forfeiture, the licence could easily be transferred to the other partner, who had three more chances.

This practice of recording the licence in one name only is noticeable in licensing records up until about the Second World War. It was taken for

Opposite: The 'Hebe' looks of Tina Gramm who was a barmaid at the Globe Hotel in Adelaide before her marriage to William Tasker, circa 1905. Photo courtesy of Genevieve Rumbelow

granted that spouses helped out but were not licensees. After the war licences tended to be granted to married couples or other types of partnerships.[3]

The attitude to women who worked or lived in hotels in the early twentieth century was a product of Victorian society where a woman's reputation was largely determined by the people she mixed with and the place where she worked. Women tended to be regarded either as angels or temptresses. Albertina Gramm, who married licensee of the Colonist and the Norwood hotels William Tasker, was a barmaid at the Globe Hotel in the city in the early 1900s when they met. An *Advertiser* article in 1959 described Albertina as once being 'a charming innocent barmaid'.[4]

Until quite recent times hotels were perceived to be male domains and few women ventured in as customers. Hotels were frequently said to be unfit places for women to work. But opinions were divided between those who believed that barmaids lowered the reputation of a hotel and those who believed it was the hotel and the male customers that ruined the barmaid. This was a constant topic of public debate. In the 1880s one chap wrote a bewildered letter to the editor of the *Advertiser* saying that 'the other day it was said it was the men who ruined the barmaids. Now ... it is the barmaids who ruin young men with their smiles.'[5]

Publicans prided themselves on carefully chosen attractive women with 'Hebe looks' as barmaids.[6] In 1880, J. McDonald of the Theatre Royal Hotel in the city said women needed other attributes beyond attractiveness. Claiming to be the largest employer of barmaids in the colony, he stated that 'a barmaid must be tolerably well educated, thoroughly trustworthy, clean and respectable, quick at reckoning, and generally of a pleasing, agreeable, and business-like disposition'.[7] Out of the many girls who applied for jobs, McDonald claimed that only one in twenty met his requirements.

While attractive barmaids were seen as a positive drawcard for any city bar, the notion of an attractive single woman applying for a publican's licence appeared to be something else altogether.

In 1852 Catherine Russell, single and seventeen-years old, was refused a licence for the Morning Star Hotel at Chain of Ponds in the Adelaide Hills. The *Register* reported that she was refused on 'account of her youth and beauty'.[8] Although there weren't many cases of this type of refusal throughout the nineteenth century, the sexual morality of women applying for a licence to manage a hotel or to work as a barmaid was under constant scrutiny. The Licensing Bench was assisted by the police in investigating the moral character of single, widowed or divorced female publicans, and barmaids were also investigated. It was not unusual for them to be made scapegoats for the worst excesses of a hotel's activities.

In the 1880s the impact of the temperance movement was evident in their campaign for prohibition. They called for stricter legislation governing the operations of hotel life.

BEHIND THE BAR OF THE NORWOOD HOTEL WITH ALBERTINA TASKER, WILLIAM TASKER AND SON CLYDE, CIRCA 1940.
PHOTO COURTESY OF GENEVIEVE RUMBELOW

From 1916 new and severely limited trading hours came into force and pubs became little more than beer sumps where women were not welcome, particularly in the front bar, as customers. In the two hours before closing time at six o'clock, the front bars were often so overcrowded that customers spilled over onto footpaths and continued drinking there. Many an old regular will wistfully testify to the many goings-on – stories mostly about men and their antics.[9] The culture of the front bar in this era only included women when they worked behind the bar either as publican, as a relative of the publican, or as a barmaid who survived from the period before the new legislation came into force.

Ironically, in a time when women had demanded equality and had lobbied successfully for the right to vote there was still active discrimination against them in hotels, on both sides of the bar. Pressure to rid the hotels of barmaids culminated in an Act of 1908 which saw only wives, mothers, sisters, daughters, or step-daughters of the licensee able to serve in front bars. This legislation gradually saw the decline in numbers of registered barmaids from over 400 to less than twenty by 1939.[10]

Although there appears to have been a rise in the number of female publicans in the mid-1890s, this was matched by increased opposition from the committee of the Licensed Victuallers' Association who were all male publicans. This association relied upon its committee to lobby the government for such issues as liquor price fixing, or amendments to the constantly changing liquor legislation. In this period the Licensed Victuallers' Association members believed that women publicans were 'tending to bring the trade into disrepute'.[11]

Accordingly, the Licensed Victuallers' Association recommended that 'searching enquiries be made as to the prospective woman publican's respectability and the manner in which she has conducted her house if she has previously held a license'.

The Act of 1908 which prohibited single women from being licensees was further amended in 1915 to class widows as single women. This ruling created much controversy, especially among those women who had helped their late husbands to run hotels. After a few cases where this ruling saw experienced women lose their livelihood on the death of their husbands, the Licensing Bench was forced to allow the transfer of licences to widows. This rule did not affect married women, who were always allowed to become publicans or assist their husbands if they wished.

The housekeeping part of a hotel remained unaffected by all these changes of legislation – women have always worked behind the scenes as cooks and maids. During the Second World War there was a critical shortage of staff in hotels so legislation was drafted to allow women to work once more behind the bar. South Australian Premier Thomas Playford objected to the new legislation on 'moral principles'. He further stated that 'it is supposed that the abolition of barmaids thirty-six years ago was a valuable moral reform and that it is a retrograde step to reintroduce barmaids'.[12]

By 1956, South Australia was the only state without barmaids, even though there was a still a critical shortage of staff in many hotels.[13] But the excesses created by six o'clock closing worked to support the claim that a hotel was no place for a woman. The bars were crowded for an hour before closing time whereupon sozzled men tottered about swearing outside the hotel giving rise to the well known expression, 'the six o'clock swill'. Perhaps Playford, 'benevolent despot' that he was, could be forgiven for preventing women from working behind the bar in this kind of environment.

During the Second World War lounge bars were a major part of a hotel's trade. Husbands brought their wives into these areas sure that front bar behaviour would not be tolerated in the lounge. Women in groups also began frequenting these lounges, including the one at the Oriental Hotel when Mary Clancey was its publican. Clancey set up a small lounge bar – sometimes called a snug – and encouraged her friends to meet there, joining them for a chat and a drink when trade was slow.[14]

Many hotels that were short of staff due to the war found a way of avoiding the prohibition on barmaids. In 1942 the Licensed Victuallers' Association argued that for 'about twenty years lounge waitresses have been permitted to serve liquor in lounges not regarded as bar rooms'. They warned their members 'that only in the last six months had police been taking action' to stamp out the practice and that there were dire consequences for those publicans caught allowing this to occur.[15]

So long as Thomas Playford was premier of South Australia it seemed that the licensing hours would never be relaxed despite constant lobbying from the liquor industry particularly in the 1950s and 1960s.[16] When Don Dunstan was elected as South Australia's Labor premier, a time of reform began in South Australia. His government soon legislated against six o'clock closing making 27 September 1967 the last day of early closing. Women were allowed to be employed in the front bars of hotels and thus hotel life changed direction overnight.

Opinions were much divided about the benefits of the new hours. For many the longer hours meant one could go home from work and stroll to the pub for an evening drink after dinner without all the desperation that six o'clock closing entailed.

The new opening times were not always popular with publicans, particularly those with young families. Mrs Moore of the Colonist Hotel was not at all impressed with 10 o'clock closing. Don Dunstan recalled, 'When I introduced the licensing act amendments in 1967, Ma Moore said to me, "Well Don, that's the finish. If there's gonna be ten o'clock closing, I'm not staying in this hotel and I'm giving it away. I've gotta have some sort of life. A publican's life if we're going to open till ten o'clock, is no life to lead, so I'm giving it away." And she did, when ten o'clock closing came in.'[17]

Relaxation of licensing regulations also saw another change. Before 1967 women were not welcome in the front bars but had right of entrance to saloon and lounge bars. Publicans recall the regulars' shock when the first women entered front bars in 1967. Macka MacKenzie of the Alma Hotel said, 'I can remember the first woman who came and sat up at the bar. Striding in boldly, she announced, "I've been wanting to do this for years," and she picked up her breasts and flopped them onto the bar.' Laughing as he recalled the occasion, Macka said that a few of the old timers propped up at the bar nearly fell off their seats with shock.[18]

THE LADIES COMMITTEE OF THE ALMA HOTEL SOCIAL CLUB.
FROM LEFT TO RIGHT: GWEN MACKENZIE, MRS CANTLON, ELAINE GANGE, JOAN SPANGLER, DOT NEVE, SHIRLEY BEBEE. CIRCA 1970. COURTESY GWEN MACKENZIE.

The end of the six o'clock swill and the reintroduction of barmaids also meant opportunities for hotels to create a more socially engaging environment – food once more became an important part of what was offered at a hotel. Counter meals had made a slow comeback since the early 1960s. Before then they were actively discouraged by absurd legislation that demanded meals be eaten in rooms away from bar areas. Before the 1960s hotel meals were in many cases little better than boarding-house fare and were provided primarily for permanent guests.

The extended licensing hours saw the development of a new and exciting hotel culture and by the 1990s many South Australian hotels became renowned for their cuisine.

CHAPTER SIX

The future of South Australian pubs

Pub culture is continually in flux. Publicans and owners need to constantly adapt to the changing demands of the public and of legislators.

THE NORWOOD HOTEL 1997. KENSINGTON & NORWOOD CIVIC COLLECTION

Hotels compete with other entertainment venues as well as with each other. There is still a belief in the general community that a hotel is not a proper place for families, so chain restaurants are formidable opponents. Some hotels, like the Marryatville, have provided children with their own play area and menu.

Although there is still a place for steak and chips in hotels, many now provide more sophisticated food at affordable prices. In doing so, they have placed themselves in competition with the many Mediterranean-style bistros with open frontages to streets and courtyards. To entice more people to eat in hotels, package deals combining food and a flutter on the pokies are offered at tiny prices. The Saturno brothers have revamped dining facilities at the Norwood Hotel several times in recent years and they expect to make continual changes to keep up with trends. All the hotels in Kensington, Norwood and Kent Town now provide bistro or restaurant facilities, each with their own stamp.

Increasing competition comes from retail liquor outlets. While townships with only one hotel might still offer healthy profits from bottle shop sales, some customers will drive further afield for discounted liquor. Most suburban hotels now have drive-in bottle shops, and some, such as the Norwood and the Colonist, have become renowned for their huge range and specialist vintages, as well as for their prices.

Clearly the days of a mine host publican who could spend many hours with his or her customers, are all but gone except in small townships. Publicans of larger hotels now must have the business skills needed to manage the several 'departments' operating under the banner of a hotel. They have to know about the complex legislation relating to the gambling facilities on their premises. They must install health and safety procedures to protect staff and clientele. They are increasingly regarded as responsible for their customers' level of intoxication. Legislation governs the total number of customers a hotel can accommodate safely, and many hotels have lost their licences for a period due to overcrowding.

Publicans also have to understand the legislation covering the employment of permanent, casual or temporary staff and deal with workcover, superannuation and leave requirements. At the same time publicans have needed to introduce a professional touch as the industry has become increasingly associated with tourism.

The publican's name is over the entrance of a hotel but regulars will more likely socialise with a manager or waiters because many publicans are increasingly trapped by administrative duties.

The popularity of the front bars is waning in the pubs of Kensington, Norwood and Kent Town. You can still drink in front bars with older folk who have been regulars for decades, but their numbers are decreasing and they are not being replaced by the next generations. Some hotels are hanging onto their front bars but others, like the Norwood Hotel, have already ousted theirs.

Although the district can boast that no hotel licence has been lost since 1909, competition from the many eating establishments on Norwood Parade and East Rundle Street makes the future unpredictable. The last ten years in the liquor industry have seen the most dramatic changes in legislation, coinciding with recession. So much so that, as one local publican remarked, 'when gaming came into hotels, probably a good seventy per cent of hotels in South Australia were trading in the red. Gaming literally picked our industry up and got it back on its feet. Without gaming, we probably wouldn't still be here.' Other hotels may have to copy the Rising Sun Inn, no longer a public house but an 'historic inn' with a restaurant licence.

Over the years owners and publicans have changed the interiors of hotels so often that the notion of a traditional pub is difficult to define. Interiors of hotels have changed from the humble 'tap room' and possibly a parlour, to the overly large bars of the six o'clock closing era, to the more comfortable bistro style environment that has become so fashionable in the 1990s.

Hotel interiors will continue to be altered and changed, and the interiors of a former era may become fashionable again. To its credit, Osmonds Hotel has retained its 1920s public bar complete with its scalloped bar mirrors. The magnificent wood-panelled front bar counter of the Kent Town Hotel captures an earlier period and so does the newer panelled bar at the Colonist. The publicans of the Kensington Hotel have maintained the pub's quieter atmosphere and interior since the 1970s, and have experienced much success.

Apart from Osmonds and the Marryatville, all the hotels trading in Kensington, Norwood and Kent Town have retained their early façades. It is ironic that, while most hotels in the district have changed unrecognisably within, their exteriors still present the image of a nineteenth-century pub.

PART TWO

KENSINGTON, NORWOOD & KENT TOWN DISTRICT HOTELS

Bath Hotel

232 THE PARADE, NORWOOD

This hotel has always been known as the Bath Hotel. In 1987 its name was changed to the Parade Tavern yet people persisted in using its former name, and the owners wisely reverted to licensing the pub as the Bath.

The first Bath Hotel was built on land that cost £100 adjacent to the present site and it opened for business on 13 March 1856. Henry Skelton, who had arrived in the colony five years before, managed the hotel until 1864, when he sub-leased it for a number of years to William Whitehorn, who bought it for his wife Emily in 1874.

It was nearly burnt down in December 1876, when the substantial Lodgeroom at the rear of the hotel caught fire causing £500 worth of damage. Fortunately the fire didn't spread to the hotel, as it took over an hour for the members of the fire brigade and a body of troopers to put in an appearance and extinguish the fire.

The Bath was rebuilt in bluestone in 1881 when it was relocated to the corner of Queen Street and the Parade replacing Arbor Cottage and its garden. The new hotel was rebuilt to a design by Thomas English for brewers Beaglehole and Johnston. From the late 1870s, breweries were locked in fierce competition buying up or leasing prominent hotels and rebuilding them in an effort to capture trade. At this time Beaglehole and Johnston also had interests in the Britannia Hotel and the newly established Oriental Hotel. Their major rival, Sir Edwin Smith of the South Australian Brewing Company, had interests in seven hotels in the council district, so it was important for Beaglehole and Johnston to compete with a substantial and showy new pub.

The breweries wanted hotels to have fine exteriors and all the dignity of a bank. Thus hotels were often relocated to prominent corner positions creating two street frontages. The 1925 verandah and balcony that once adorned both façades of the Bath Hotel were partly demolished in the late 1950s when the council decided they were a menace to buses and lorries.

Like many hotels, the Bath provided clubroom accommodation until March 1916 – when six o'clock closing was introduced – for some of the organisations of the district that were exclusive to men. The Kensington branch of the Ancient Order of Foresters began meeting there in 1858 and the East Torrens Lodge was established there in 1877.

A hotel's character was strongly influenced by its publican, as is illustrated by the case of Edward Baker who was mine host at the Bath Hotel between 1901 and 1926. Coming from the Kapunda district in the mid-north where he had won numerous trophies for athletics, Baker transferred his interest from two-legged to four-legged racing when he became a successful horse breeder and racehorse owner. He owned the Bath Hotel

Bath Hotel in 1900 before addition of balcony and verandah.
Photo courtesy of Tony Franzon

briefly before selling it and buying the Erinvale Stud Farm at Salisbury which he kept until his death in 1936.

The hotel's popularity during Baker's reign was noticed in 1909 when hotels were being assessed for the Local Option Polls. While five local hotels lost their licences, it was reported that the Bath Hotel was considered one of

Don Mewett, a speed cop before he became publican of the Bath Hotel between 1967 and 1977.
Photo courtesy of Deborah Mewett

the best in the suburbs. Furthermore, the Licensing Bench noticed that it was catering for the sporting community – footballers from the Norwood Football Club socialised there with their fans. Baker's popularity and success in the trade were obviously something his children wanted to emulate for his daughter Constance and a son Lance both chose careers as publicans.

At some point after the Bakers' departure, the hotel lost its sporting clientele. But in 1959 incoming publican Lance Thyer and his wife Pat changed the hotel's character overnight. Pat, who had hardly ever been in a hotel lounge in her life, let alone pulled a beer, came to love the life and 'chatting with the men'. The Thyers, in their seven years at the Bath, opened every morning at six to serve hot coffee with rum, very welcome on a cold early morning for those returning from night shift or going to work.

When Lance became involved with the Norwood Football Club, the hotel once more became home to the local football fraternity. Many early discussions about the building of the football club's premises took place at the Bath. Football supporters drank there before a local match and returned there afterwards with their heroes. Referred to as 'Mum' by the footballers, Pat Thyer said that after a win they would return to the hotel, grab her in their arms and whirl her into the air with glee shouting, 'We've won again Mum, we've won!'

After such wins six o'clock closing was ignored. Celebrations continued in the dining room with hotel barmaid May Attrill pulling the beers alongside the barmen even though it was not strictly legal for a woman to do bar work. Pat Thyer admitted 'I don't know how we got away with it, but she did it all the time we were there'.

May was the hotel treasure. She lived on the premises, was treated like one of the family and excelled at one particular duty for many years. She was the hotel bookie, responsible for all the hotel's betting and with her own 'nit-keepers' who warned of approaching police. Pat added cheekily that despite these activities, 'I don't know that Lance ever did get a stroke [conviction] against him.'

The Bath was very much a family hotel, and for seven years the Thyers lived on the premises with their two children and a host of other characters including a bank employee called Elliott, three Victorian footballers transferred to the Norwood Football team for several years, and May. Later, according to long time regular Dennis O'Donoghue, the Norwood Football Club used the hotel to accommodate their young country recruits.

Don Mewett, former policeman and a barman for the Thyers, took over the licence of the hotel in September 1967 when the licensing hours were extended from six to ten o'clock closing. It appeared that the clientele stayed on, as did May Attrill. Mewett's friend and former colleague, Kevin Shannon, worked for him part-time for ten years and described his friend as a 'spot on sort of bloke'. Mewett always wore a collar and tie, and Kevin mischievously suggested that he probably dressed up to go fishing.

During this time at the Bath Hotel fifty or more Italians, who worked mainly in the building trade, started to make the Bath their local. They all came from the same part of Italy and Kevin said they were a 'good mob of people' of all ages who all ragged each other and him.

These Italian workmen became a welcome part of the hotel clientele as did members of the Juventus soccer team, now known as Adelaide City, who 'never drank beer because it blew them up too much' and so drank Creme de Menthe instead.

Kev Shannon said that during this period he used to make a quid on the side from one of the soccer players who could do an amazing trick. The Bath at that time had one of the highest bars in the neighbourhood but the soccer player could leap from the ground onto the bar with his arms folded. To encourage the sceptics to bet, the soccer player would slip a few times before performing a perfect leap onto the bar.

Even with the changes of publicans the hotel has retained several regulars including Keith Aplin who was a customer for at least fifty years. If he didn't turn up on any particular day, someone would nip down to his place to see if he was all right. Another regular has proved that if you hang about long enough, your knowledge of the pub becomes so valuable to an incoming publican that you become the unofficial 'Boots' of the hotel. This is what happened to Dennis O'Donoghue. He knows what he's talking about when he says that while the front bar is still a feature of the Bath Hotel, generally its popularity is waning, mainly because of the changing clientele.

For the last ten years the reins of the Bath Hotel have been held by George Franzon and his son Tony who says that the change in the liquor industry has been drastic, especially over the last four years. 'I don't look at a hotel as a local pub anymore. Hotels must now be entertainment centres with substantial and affordable restaurant facilities,' he says.

For about eight years the Bath was the home of the Rostrevor Old Collegians Club known as the Rocs Club which was sponsored by the present-day publicans. Even though the hotel has been modernised, the Bath has kept its substantial front bar and, because of the hotel's popularity, the Franzons have not needed to look beyond the local district for their clientele.

Britannia Hotel

1 KENSINGTON ROAD, NORWOOD

The Britannia Hotel, with its fine cast-iron lace verandah and balcony, is a landmark structure to all drivers converging at one of Adelaide's most bewildering traffic hazards, the Britannia roundabout.

For most of its history this hotel has been associated with the 'sport of kings' – horseracing. It opened on a prominent corner in June 1850 when Norwood was first subdivided and has remained on the site ever since. The early one-storey hotel on one acre included eight rooms. It was located on a main road to the village of Kensington and was also close to the Victoria Park racecourse. The hotel was rebuilt in 1882 but the cast-iron lace verandah and balcony were not added until 1925.

TO BE SOLD

THE Lease and Good Will, Furniture, and Fixtures of that newly built Public House, called the Britannia Hotel, corner of Norwood, adjoining the Park Land, and facing the Race Course.

The Lease is twenty years unexpired.

For particulars apply on the Premises, or to

W. H. CLARK, Esq.,
Clark's Buildings, Hindley-street.
Norwood, Jan. 10, 1851.

LEASE ADVERTISEMENT, ADELAIDE *TIMES* 11 JANUARY 1851

The Britannia's proximity to one of Adelaide's most popular sporting venues attracted owners and licensees who were either trainers, owners of horses or retired jockeys. In 1879 the licensee, William Rusbridge, advertised his excellent stable accommodation for trainers. In the same decade the Adelaide Hunt Club often began their meets at the hotel, moving off across the parklands and vacant suburban properties in pursuit of rabbits.

The racing tradition continued well into the twentieth century. Lloyd Skinner, licensee during the Second World War, was a keen racing man. Once he visited Melbourne and returned with a racehorse, Lamarus, which had competed in the Australian Cup. Although Skinner had never intended buying the horse, he succumbed when a well-known sportsman known as E. Eccles offered it at a bargain price. He also owned a horse called Garfield that was named after his son.

In the war years Skinner and his partner in business, Florence Goyder, were so popular that the Britannia burst at the seams between five and six o'clock every weeknight and on Saturday afternoons. The hotel was even more crowded on race days. But the Britannia couldn't cope with the huge crowds; its internal spaces had not been adapted for the six o'clock closing rush. Customers waited to be served in a crush three or four deep. While the licensing inspector described the bars as 'old fashioned', the thirsty customers complained and demanded better facilities. 'Installation of a modern island bar and up-to-date saloon bar would be more in keeping with the requirements of the large number of quite good class customers using this hotel from Norwood, Kent Town and Rose Park,' suggested the hotel inspector. After lengthy negotiations between the licensees and the owners, who were the five sisters in the Tothill family, approval was given by the Licensing Bench to renovate the main bar by removing the passage wall and installing an island bar. The dining room was also converted into a saloon bar.

The Britannia Hotel. Artist Arthur Wilson, 1976

Even after these costly renovations some nearby residents were not happy. The refurbishments had not included adequate urinals for the crowds of male customers. The manager of a nearby service station was furious that customers used the hedge running along his service station boundary as well as the wall of his home under his windows, and even the nearby telephone box. The problem was even worse when soldiers frequented the hotel but he noticed that there were no problems when a policeman was about. He suggested that if new lavatories couldn't be built then at least the paddock behind the hotel should be made accessible.

Since those heady war days and six o'clock closing, the hotel's facilities have dramatically improved under entrepreneurial owners Chris Angelopoulos and his son, Con. Chris has owned the hotel for twenty-five years. He completed some renovations on 10 July 1996 that created a one-stop entertainment complex the 'Roundabout gaming and bistro' that includes a courtyard. The hotel is a popular lunching spot for many businesses in the area while customers from all over Adelaide come to use the entertainment facilities. Regulars from the local area who have been coming to the hotel for years continue to frequent the front bar. To retain the heritage aspects of the hotel the Angelopouloses have kept the front bar as it was.

The Colonist Tavern

44 THE PARADE, NORWOOD

Affectionately known as 'Old Col' and built in stages, there are parts to the rear of the hotel that date from 1851. The hotel, first licensed as the Old Colonist, was built as a one-storey structure of six rooms and a bar on almost four acres of land. It began trading from 3 April 1851, with Frederick Hobbs as first owner and publican.

Hobbs had friends in high places, and he managed to borrow £450 from Sir George Maclean of Hobart who was then Commissioner General for Van Diemen's Land. The contract specified that the loan was to be paid back by March 1856, but perhaps with distance came neglect. After Maclean's death in 1861, and during the lengthy probate period which dragged on until 1873, it was discovered that Hobbs had never honoured the agreement. He had sold the hotel in 1855 for £700, making a handsome profit, and moved onto greener pastures.

In 1872, when brewer Edwin Smith was leasing the hotel and had agreed to pay architects Thomas English and Rowland Rees £300 for renovations, the demand for repayment of the loan surfaced. Smith graciously repaid the loan to Maclean's widow, Lady Sarah, who was then living in the Channel Islands. Then he promptly set about suing Hobbs. Having cured the hotel's financial hiccups before actually buying it, Smith added the Old Colonist to his large collection of hotels. He gave the building a new front six years later. This new façade was described by the *Licensed Victuallers' Gazette* as 'representing a striking contrast to the unpretentious structure that formerly existed at the corner of the Sydenham Road'. A second storey was added about 1911 and other additions and remodellings which included a balcony and verandah, continued until 1928. These also included two-storey additions which were built along the Sydenham Street frontage. The verandah and balcony, like part of the balcony of the Bath Hotel, were removed in about 1954.

The Old Colonist in the 1970s. Kensington & Norwood Civic Collection

The hotel, which now has a richly panelled 1980s bar and counter, once had a bar that can only be described as a treasure lost. During the 1879 renovations the *Licensed Victuallers' Gazette* described the bar as 'one of the most commodious in the Adelaide district, with an elegant and substantial counter of cedar; revelled with panels of Huon pine'. During these same renovations a new billiard table from Melbourne was installed. This was a guaranteed crowd-puller that publican Thomas Born had brought back with him after attending the Melbourne Cup. Apparently it was one of the 'most handsome if not the handsomest billiard table in South Australia, the massive framework is built entirely of blackwood and made by well known Victorian makers Alcock & Co'. The table was set in its own room, which was 'lofty, spacious, well lighted and supplied with every convenience [which] will doubtless prove a pleasant lounge for the lovers of the game resident in the vicinity'. With all the razzamatazz that surrounded the launching of a ship, the billiard table was christened with opening games played by 'the principal knights of the cue, both amateur and professional' according to the *Licensed Victuallers' Gazette* on 2 December 1879.

After the introduction of six o'clock closing, the Bath and the Colonist Hotel seemed to have gained a reputation. They were regularly under the eye of the Norwood police, perhaps more so than any other pub in the district. In fact, until recently the Colonist had the most colourful reputation of any hotel in the district and many rollicking tales have emerged. One event which took place in the late 1950s or early 1960s inspired the plot of an episode in a television series.

The incident involved the hotel's fiery redheaded licensee, Euphemia Agnes Moore, affectionately known as Ma, her barman, known as Flash, and their defence lawyer, Don Dunstan, who later became premier of South Australia. The allegation was that Ma and Flash were caught unlawfully gambling in the pub. But it turned out that this was all a matter of interpretation and the police and the accused saw matters differently.

The police alleged that they had seen money and chits changing hands. Adding further weight to the allegations was the fact that the races were always on on the wireless. Based on what they had seen, the police charged the licensee and her barman with unlawful gaming in a hotel. But when the case came before the court everything was easily explained and there were many witnesses eager to testify that Mrs Moore often helped out those who were down on their luck and needed a little cash to tide them over. Apparently she did this by exchanging IOUs for money. The man in the blazer who had been handed a sum of money was in fact accepting payment for wood he had supplied.

When the police claimed they had seen many other suspicious things happening from a particular vantage point, barrister Don Dunstan took the magistrate to the spot and proved that it could not have been possible to see these things. With no betting slips or other betting paraphernalia in evidence, the case was dismissed and the jubilant party retired to the Brecknock Hotel near the courthouse for 'much joy and celebration'.

Flash, eternally grateful, always turned up thereafter to hand out 'how to vote' cards for Don's election days. Mrs Moore and Flash said that they would spread the word that 'Don had seen that justice was done'. The case was used as the basis of one of the episodes of the television series *Carson's Law*. Don Dunstan, as one of the consultants for the series, wrote several plots based on cases he'd been involved in which were then scripted to suit the era in which the series was set.

GEORGE SORRELL,

(Late of Foundry Hotel, Hindley -st.),

HAS TAKEN THE

OLD COLONIST INN,

NORWOOD.

PRIMROSE'S SUPERIOR ALES.

Large Billiard Room fitted with one of Alcock's Exhibition Tables. Efficient Marker.

Public Catering as heretofore attended to.

Advertising the new billiard room. *Licensed Victuallers' Gazette* 9 December 1881

Shirley Stott Despoja, one-time reporter for the Adelaide *Advertiser*, interviewed some of the Colonist's regulars in the lounge of the hotel in February 1985. She captured much of the hotel's relaxed atmosphere and the type of clientele it then attracted which was mainly working class. The regulars in the lounge were quick to refer to the front bar as 'low life', while calling the lounge 'medium life'. Then they made it clear to Despoja that they always drank in the front bar.

Incoming publican Heinz Keimeier, who took over the hotel in 1996, was well aware of the hotel's legacies – its resident ghost and its pokie machines. While he is preparing to relocate the machines away from the main body of the hotel, to emphasise that the main core of the business is food and drink, he is not about to try ridding the hotel of the ghost. There are two lots of old beer bottles that are carefully dusted and turned daily as part of the mandatory chores. Failure to do this little chore, he and his staff have found, can result in strange happenings. Heinz claims to be a sceptic but he isn't about to let the bottles get dusty.

Kensington Hotel

23 REGENT STREET, KENSINGTON

The Kensington Hotel has changed very little over the many years it has been tucked away in a quiet corner of Kensington. Its almost secret location means perhaps even some Kensington residents haven't yet discovered its whereabouts. This pub's old-fashioned feel and location make it essentially 'a local pub' and this is much appreciated by its mainly older clientele.

The present publican, David Pink, speaks fondly of two groups that have used the hotel since before he took over in May 1989. One is an old-time dancing club. Although its meetings moved off the premises some years back, original members book in every Saturday night for dinner as the 'dance group'. The hotel's other group is its Golf Club which regularly goes away at weekends to play different courses.

While he and his wife run the hotel as the 'cosy little local', David Pink freely admits that the introduction of a few discreet pokie machines has 'literally picked our industry up and got it back on its feet. Without gaming, we probably wouldn't be here'. Despite the machines, he emphasises that 'we probably get more satisfaction and more enjoyment out of running the hotel as a hotel. We feel we are hoteliers, not gambling operators.'

The hotel has had a reputation for its local feel since at least the late 1970s and early 1980s. At that time the hotel was very special to a coterie of men who met there every lunchtime and evening for conversation and companionship. One was a well driller, one went on to become a pig farmer, three were brothers who worked in banks and the one who told me of these 'most enjoyable times' worked for an advertising agency. These friends looked forward equally to seeing each other and to the interaction with the bar staff. Arthur Wilson of this group recalls days when the only noise to be heard in the hotel was the sound of voices deep in conversation and the clink of glasses. But the hotel's recent quiet character is in contrast to its colourful past.

The Kensington Hotel is the district's oldest pub, but the present 1882 building is the third one on the site. The hotel licence dates back to1840. From this licence both the present Kensington and Robin Hood hotels share the same history between 1840 and 1849. The present hotel has been known by several names, making its history complex. It was the Kensington Arms from 1840 to 1842, the Robin Hood between 1846 and 1849 and the Globe between 1849 and 1958. Since then, it has been known as the Kensington Hotel. However, between 1882 and 1909 there was another hotel in the district called the Kensington Hotel, which was on Shipsters Road, just to confuse the issue even more.

KENSINGTON ARMS INN Village of Kensington, one and a half miles from Adelaide. J. SCOTT begs leave to inform his Friends and the public, that he has opened the above Inn in this delightful and rising village, where they will find every accommodation on moderate terms.

Wines, spirits, and malt liquors of the very best quality.

A general store is also attached, where provisions &c., may be obtained, which to those living in the country will be found an accommodation.

South Australian Register
4 April 1840

The original Kensington Arms had one of fifty-three licences granted across South Australia in 1840. Only about a dozen of that number are still operating, including the present Kensington Hotel and its nearest competitor in the 1840s, the Woodforde Arms, now known as the Tower Hotel on Magill Road. Before the licences for 1840 were granted there were about sixty hotels scattered around the colony.

The Kensington Arms, described in the Kensington and Norwood Council's *50 Years of Kensington and Norwood* as 'merely a mud hut', was advertised in April 1840 by Henry Scott, who had opened the hotel in the 'delightful and rising village', with a well-stocked general store attached. Only two weeks before Scott officially relinquished his licence on 31 March 1841, his hotel was robbed late at night by four masked men. Luckily for Scott he was not there but the incoming licensees, Thomas Ball and his wife, were. There to learn the ropes, they must have wondered whether it was such a delightful place after they were assaulted and tied up. Then the robbers 'shouted' themselves at the bar before heading off in the direction of The Tiers in the Adelaide Hills with whatever valuables they could carry.

It wasn't long before the zealous Alexander Tolmer, policeman extraordinaire, was on their trail with his troopers. After Mrs Ball had shown him the break-in point where there was a footprint showing differing nails in the sole of the boot of one of the robbers, Tolmer and his men tracked the

KENSINGTON HOTEL 1998.
PHOTOGRAPHED BY TREVOR FOX.
KENSINGTON & NORWOOD
CIVIC COLLECTION

villains into the hills. They discovered the wrenched off heel-piece of the boot along a hill track. Tolmer led his men 'towards certain huts' where several 'rough cut-throat looking rascals' were found relaxing, including the one with the missing heel. With such conclusive evidence, Tolmer drew his sword and arrested them. The leader of the gang, Joseph Storey, was initially given the death sentence but this was commuted to transportation for life in August 1841. One member of the gang was acquitted while the other two later escaped from the Adelaide Gaol.

It is not certain what immediate effect the robbery had on the new licensees or the hotel's trade but on 8 June 1842 L.O. Butler took over the licence very briefly before going out of business. Three years later the property was sold to brothers Robert and Richard Pepperell for £200. The Kensington Arms hotel may have been forced out of business after a city publican named John Wheland opened a hotel called the Catherine Wheel in August 1842 on the three-way corner of Norwood Parade, Hill and Bridge streets where it operated until 1846.

When the Catherine Wheel closed, the former Kensington Arms was revamped and relicensed on 9 March 1846 and changed its name to the Robin Hood. William Beck, 'a man of colour', usually a polite term for a negro, was its publican. What type of friends he entertained is not known but when the hotel's opening night celebrations landed him in court a few days later he was fined two guineas for 'on the occasion of his opening entertainment, he had admitted loose and bad characters about his house'.

A year later, in June 1847 Beck's licence was extended when Thomas Tasker's application for a licence to open a new hotel in the district was knocked back because the male population of the village was less than forty and considered too small a community to support another hotel. Determined to operate his own hotel, Tasker was able to persuade Beck to transfer his licence to him six months later. But within two years, when the subdivision of Norwood was underway, Tasker tried to transfer the licence to William Akehurst of Bowden.

Akehurst had invested £250 for a fourteen-year lease on the hotel property. But unexpectedly, at the licensing hearing, he was accused of being a Van Diemen's Land convict and the licence was refused. Members of the Licensing Bench were kept informed by the Colonial Secretary in Van Diemen's Land of 'certain classes of persons leaving there for other colonies'. Although Akehurst denied being a convict, the next day when he presented himself back at the licensing court with references, the bench members announced that all his referees were convicts too, even though they had all done their time. At the hearing the question was put as to 'whether we are to have convicts or not for publicans?' For Akehurst, the outcome was bleak. He was stuck with a fourteen-year lease on a building from which he could not make a living.

With settlement of Norwood imminent, Thomas Tasker was finally allowed to transfer the licence of the first Robin Hood Hotel to its second site on the Portrush Road in March 1851. Meanwhile, the old Kensington Arms hotel on the corner of Regent and Thornton streets was rebuilt by owners Richard and Robert Pepperell who had bought the property in 1845. After it was rebuilt in 1849 it became the Globe Hotel, a name it retained until 1958. In 1854 it was described as having seven rooms and a stable on one acre.

Many hotels by the 1880s were either leased or bought by breweries. In April 1881, the Globe was leased to Alfred Simms who, in March 1882, commissioned architects Thomas English and George Soward to design a new twenty-one room hotel. Six years later it was sold to the South Australian Brewing Company which owned the hotel until 1984.

Kent Town Hotel

76 RUNDLE STREET, KENT TOWN

This hotel is a significant landmark in Kent Town. It dates back to 1856, shortly after the township was first subdivided. A substantial building, the eleven-room one-storey hotel was run in its first year by owner William Henry Sims. He then sublet it to a well-known Adelaide publican named James Chittleborough, a pioneer who came to South Australia on the ship *Buffalo.* Chittleborough had previously opened one of the colony's first hotels, a tent in the parklands that he called the Buffalo's Head.

Chittleborough was in the hotel trade all his life and was at one time chairman of the Licensed Victuallers' Association. When he was publican of the Kent Town Hotel he was mine host at an important testimonial dinner held in April 1859 for the explorer John McDouall Stuart. As well as dinners such as this, the hotel was a meeting place for several men's organisations such as the Duke of Kent Lodge and the Kent Town Rifle Corps.

Unlike many other hotels in the district, the Kent Town hotel was never owned by a brewing company. For the longest part of its existence between 1855 and 1921 it was owned by a butcher, William Henry Sims and his family. Unlike other privately owned hotels in the district, such as the Vintage Shades and Family Hotel, Sims knew when to update his hotel in order to keep up with his brewery competitors. In 1881 he commissioned the best known hotel architects of the day, Thomas English and George Soward, to design a new hotel. It was built by Stepney contractor Charles Lidbury, for £3000. After its completion, the *Licensed Victuallers' Gazette* stated that Sims was 'alive to the requirement today' for he had rebuilt the hotel 'much larger and with more internal comfort than the old one'. The balcony was not added until over forty years later in 1925 when the hotel was renovated by new owners, Sydney and Gilbert Johns.

Gilbert became publican for fourteen years until 1938. Like many publicans, Gilbert had an interest in sports. He was an expert in game shooting and he also took part in coursing. Together with his dog Alec he would often join Max Flannagan of the Norfolk Hotel, with his dog Snap, and Bill Quigley of the Avenues Hotel in Stepney. Each Thursday, summer and winter, they would leave town long before dawn and be back for breakfast with as many as seventy birds at a time. In the early 1930s the trio were reported to have bagged a thousand birds in one season. Sometimes they took longer trips to the Coorong.

The Kent Town Hotel in 1912 before the present verandah and balcony were added.
Kensington & Norwood Civic Collection

Frederick Clarke, who was publican of the Kent Town Hotel from 1905 until 1912, was described by the newspaper *Quiz* as an expert swimmer. In September 1909 he was recognised for having invented a life-jacket that was the most 'up-to-date appliance ever used to save a life'. Between 1900 and 1910, Clarke and partner J. Aistrope appear to have patented several variations of 'a collapsible life-saving jacket' as well as a 'portable five-barrelled rifle'.

Hotels go through periods of prosperity and decline depending on owners, publicans and the economy. Ownership of the Kent Town Hotel was transferred to the trustees after the death of Gilbert Johns in 1943, and the pub's trade became run-down. In 1960 incoming publican Donald Scott, often known as Scotty, thought that the Kent Town had great potential. When he became publican the hotel had plain-coloured cement-rendered façades with bright red painted detailing, lino on the floors and glossy painted walls. But under his careful management the hotel went through a quiet and steady renaissance that was the prerequisite for its present day popularity.

Scott soon found out that he was risking more than his money by taking on a run-down pub with a reputation to match. But he didn't mind the occasional scrap, if it meant ridding the hotel of its more unsavoury characters, including a couple of unwanted SP bookies.

Scott worked to make the pub respectable for its close-knit clientele, who were mostly working-class residents and shift workers from the Kent Town Maltings. When the shift workers came into the hotel at six in the morning they drank hot toddies made from a teaspoon of Bovril mixed with hot water and a tot of rum.

Because of the hotel's reputation, Scott had to operate under the watchful eye of two policemen, who would appear daily at closing time and stand by with folded arms. Their presence made sure no sip was drunk past six o'clock, which often frustrated attempts to serve the final round of drinks to a group of customers. Rounds were left unpaid as no money could change hands after the stroke of six. Customers who missed out on receiving their last beer expressed their bitter disappointment which could also generate much jocularity. After being caught out a number of times, Scott learned not to take an order if he knew the transaction could not be completed before the hands of the clock landed dead on six o'clock.

The first year of ten o'clock closing was a disaster to Scott's trade. Few of his evening customers could afford to continue drinking after six. In 1968 he applied for, and was granted, a licence to continue trading very much as he did before late closing was introduced. As it turned out he need not have worried. The increasing numbers of commercial houses in Kent Town saw his lunchtime clientele grow, especially when he began providing Gibbs' pies and pasties in 1969.

Trade at the Kent Town Hotel really took off from the day Donald Scott placed a piece of metal over his open fire in the bar and threw on some chops and sausages. The primitive cooking facilities were immediately taken in hand by his thoughtful regulars, who thought they could improve the barbecue. One provided a large cast iron grate from a demolition job in

North Adelaide and put it into the cracked and fretting fireplace. Another regular then produced a heavy metal hot plate made by one of his apprentices at a trade school. When the chops ran out, his customers nipped to the nearby butcher shop and bought their own. Before he knew it, it became the trend for customers to buy chops and 'snags' and bring them back to barbecue. They never paid for using the barbecue facilities, but they did need drinks to wash the meal down. Scott's barbecue was among the first of its kind in the state, a predecessor to the very popular barbecue meals that customers paid to cook themselves from the late 1970s in hotels around the city. For Donald Scott, trade roared from the time he provided the original hot plate.

As a publican with 'attitude', he knew how to stand up for himself and his fellow publicans. After ten o'clock closing was introduced the next big challenge was Sunday trading. Scott believed that the hotels should stay shut. Like anyone else, publicans were entitled to a day off to spend with their families. Scott believed that publicans around the state were of a like mind, and he wrote to every one of them to gauge their views. He was not surprised to find that he had overwhelming support. Armed with all the letters, Scott attended a crucial meeting of the South Australian Hotels' Association (formerly the Licensed Victuallers' Association) where a vote was to be taken. His evidence proved beyond a doubt the power of the small publicans when they clubbed together. However, after he left the trade, Sunday trading was introduced.

The hotel has continued to be a popular lunchtime watering hole for the many businesses in the area. Recently a magnificent, almost circular, timber-panelled bar and counter was installed and is now the major feature in the front bar.

For a time from the early 1980s Barry Ion, of Baz and Pilko radio fame, had an interest in the hotel. From August 1996 the hotel was in the capable hands of Rick Panizza, the son of a publican who once ran the now demolished Centralia Hotel on North Terrace. Providing a lush courtyard in which to linger on warmer days and a pot belly stove to warm up the dining areas in winter, Rick pitched his trade to the twenty-five to fifty-five year olds, including the semi-professionals and small business people working in the area. With an emphasis on service and quality at a reasonable price, his hotel provided bistro meals and gaming facilities.

Marryatville Hotel

☚ 239 KENSINGTON ROAD, KENSINGTON ☛

For many years during and after the Second World War, there was always a certain atmosphere at the Marryatville Hotel, which catered for middle-class locals wanting to feel as though they were at home. It also became a local saying that 'if you want a good drink of beer go out to the Marryatville'.

For a hotel that provided no entertainment or food and where no local organisations or societies met, the beer, served in a dignified atmosphere, represented ninety-five per cent of the Marryatville's trade. Its reputation for the best fresh sweet beer, which many travelled to sample, was earned by publican Horrie Yeoman and his son Max's laborious evening ritual of thoroughly flushing out the copper pipes. The pipes were then soaked for the night before another flushing in the morning before opening time.

The hotel's up-market reputation survived the war when it became a favourite watering hole for interstate soldiers billeted in the district. The soldiers were generally mischievous, unruly and noisy, but their presence, according to Mrs Githa Yeoman, created 'a sort of very warm feeling right throughout the district'. The soldiers that made the hotel their second home accepted the high standards of behaviour and fell in line with the publican's expectations. When the soldiers eventually left Mrs Yeoman missed the life they brought to the hotel, while Max said he missed the takings.

When Max began running the hotel with his father he wanted, like the Thyers at the Bath Hotel, to ward off the 'winey' clientele. He disconnected the draught wine lines and tipped the cheap 'plonk' down the drain. Wine was then served by the glass from bottles.

The history of the Marryatville Hotel dates back to 17 June 1857. It was

The Marryatville hotel, circa 1882. SLSA: MLSA B9710

established on the corner of Kensington and Clapton roads, the site of the first Marryatville police station. It quickly became a 'favourite with the woodcarters, who necessarily passed it on their way downwards from the ranges'. Brewer Edwin Smith recognised the hotel's potential to fit in with his own plans so he bought it and transferred the licence.

Meanwhile, in December 1880, the Adelaide and Suburban Tramway Company bought Lots 63, 77 and 64 across the road, on the corner of High Street, Shipsters and Kensington roads, for a tram terminus, selling Lot 64 to Smith. In a smart move to catch the new trade, Smith rebuilt the hotel in 1880 and 1881 next-door to the tram terminus.

The new hotel was designed by prominent architect Rowland Rees, who was known for the rich detailing on his designs. The twenty-seven room hotel cost £3500, and was built by R. Honey. In February 1883 publican Mrs Rachel Hince advertised that the hotel 'embraces a magnificent view of the Mount Lofty ranges, and is a most desirable residence all the year around'. The advert also emphasised that the 'tramcars pass the door every five minutes'.

Between 1936 and 1937 the old cast-iron balcony was removed and a concrete balcony was added to both frontages, emphasising the building's size.

Incoming publican Len Williams, who took over the hotel in 1955 and stayed for twenty-two years, set about modernising the hotel again in 1959. In November of that year, the Mayor of Kensington and Norwood was invited to open the 'amazing transformation'. The 'old style front bar' had been replaced with a 'modern central saloon and elaborate cocktail bars'. The spacious, renovated lounge seated 150 guests, while the new beer garden held a further 200 people. The latest refrigeration plants of the day were in place, and they could store 2000 dozen bottles in the new drive-in bottle shop. In declaring the hotel open, Mayor Fred McCallum said that the hotel was 'now not only a credit to the hotel industry in South Australia, but more particularly, from the council's point of view, a wonderful attraction to the city of Kensington and Norwood'.

Keeping up with the times almost forty years on, the Marryatville has been transformed into a family hotel where children's needs are catered for with their own special menus and a glassed-in courtyard complete with playground. Parents can eat, drink, and be entertained in peace.

The Marryatville Hotel showing the remodelled verandah and balcony, 1946.
Photo courtesy of Rita Fox

New Alma Hotel

(FORMERLY THE ALMA HOTEL)

66 MAGILL ROAD, NORWOOD

This hotel was named after a battle that took place around the Alma River in 1854 during the Crimean War. The battle of the year before was still topical when the hotel first opened in June 1855. The Alma was built amid a village community that had settled around this early part of Norwood in humble two and three-roomed dwellings. The first Alma hotel, with its outbuildings and extra land, reflected the humble working-class nature of the surroundings.

The first publican, Robert Standley, who owned several small cottages adjacent to the pub and also operated a blacksmith's forge, had bought the vacant corner lot in January 1854. A year later he borrowed £150 from Edward Stirling and built a hotel, however, within nine months of its opening he leased it and moved to Eyre Peninsula to become a farmer.

After Standley's death in 1890, his family sold the hotel in 1895 to James Pinchbeck, who came from a well-known family of hoteliers. The Pinchbecks honoured the existing thirty-year lease agreement with brewer Edwin Smith, who had been leasing the hotel since 1875 and had partially rebuilt it in 1878 to a design by Thomas English. After Pinchbeck died, it wasn't Smith's South Australian Brewing Company that bought the Alma in 1903 but another brewer, Charles Mallen. After his death the Mallen family owned it until the late 1970s.

The Alma was the first of the early one-storey hotels in the district to add a storey during the colony's nineteenth century building boom. At the same time, in 1878, the new Adelaide and Suburban Tramway Company's first line was routed to Kensington. The tracks went along Norwood Parade via

THE NEW ALMA HOTEL, 1998. PHOTOGRAPHED BY TREVOR FOX. KENSINGTON & NORWOOD CIVIC COLLECTION

Sydenham Road and Beulah Road to the city. The other line, the East Adelaide and Maylands service, passed the hotel as it travelled along Magill Road to Magill from 1882.

Thomas Pegler was the Alma's publican when an extra eight rooms were added to the existing ten in 1878. Most likely it was these additions that transformed the hotel into the present two-storey building. It is quite possible that there are remnants of the earlier 1850s hotel to be found on the ground floor. The additions, as noted by the *Licensed Victuallers' Gazette*, made the hotel 'one of the most comfortable quarters one would wish to inhabit'. One of the additions was a large assembly room, which was the largest in Norwood and suitable for such events as public meetings. The hotel gazette stated that 'inside and outside, the Alma presents a really nice appearance, everything bespeaking cleanliness and order', and that sojourners would find the comforts of the best of homes.

Tom Pegler, the publican of the transformed hotel, had spent twenty years at the Brecknock Hotel in the city before taking over the lease of the Alma in September 1871. When he died in November 1883, at just forty-five, his widow Elizabeth Sarah continued the business for a number of years. After she married William O'Brien, the licence continued in the O'Brien name from 1888 until 1895.

Despite a conviction against him in 1878 for supplying drink to an intoxicated person, for which he was fined ten pounds, Pegler became president of the Licensed Victuallers' Association for two years until March 1883. His obituary in the association's gazette eulogised his 'zeal and energy on behalf of the trade'. While described as 'not a brilliant man', he was remembered as 'a thorough unselfish one who could be depended upon to work when work needed doing'.

In recent times, the Alma was like the family home to a group of regulars. So complete was their devotion to the hotel that, when an outgoing publican went on to become bar manager at the Oriental in 1967, they stayed on at the Alma with their new publican, the very jovial Macka MacKenzie. In the mistaken belief that the regulars were loyal to him, the outgoing publican told Macka, 'You'll lose half your customers.' Macka said that it wasn't just his popularity that held the regulars, the glue cementing them to the Alma was the extraordinarily lively Alma Social Club, which was formed out of the hotel's cricket club about 1958 and lasted into the early 1980s. The Alma numbers were also swollen by customers who followed MacKenzie from the Edinburgh Hotel at Mitcham. They also became involved in the social club, and grew used to the lively regulars bearing nicknames like Spoggy, Clacka and Pinky.

MacKenzie moved into a hotel where wives and children were very much part of the scene, thanks to the social club. At Christmas parties men

Members of the Alma Hotel's social club in 1970, (from left) Ray Gange, barman; Bill (Pinky) Evans, John (Spoggy) Spangler, John (Butch) Cantlon; Stan (Chinaman) Neve; 'Macka' MacKenzie, Alan Brennan and John (Araldite) Bebee. Photo courtesy of Alan Brennan

dressed up as women to perform for the adults. Cabarets, trips and picnics were held regularly. The sixty-forty music provided for the mature clientele kept out the teenagers who preferred music to match their age. A children's party, held each year for approximately a hundred youngsters on a nearby oval, was one of the highlights. Father Christmas gave every child a present that had been specially chosen. The social club, which also raised money for charity, was so active that there was a ladies' committee as well as a men's committee responsible for organising events.

Macka MacKenzie was born in a pub into a hotel family. When asked what he'd do if he could have his life over again, he said, 'It was a great life. If I had my life again, I'd still be a publican, but only there at the Alma at the same time with that clientele.' But Macka's time at the Alma was just one period in the hotel's long history.

Now the hotel is under the management of Ian Menzies and Phil Moore. The New Alma successfully caters for a good cross-section of people of all ages. The inexpensive bistro attracts a mainly mature clientele, while the twenty to thirty-year-olds are entertained by a DJ twice a week and by eight ball tables. Ian says, 'You'd be surprised how many girls play eight ball.' There are two dozen pokie machines in one part of the hotel, but Ian says that the front bar clientele are happy about the absence of TAB or Keno facilities. They can chat and concentrate on their eight ball.

Dancing girls of the Alma Hotel Social Club Christmas Party, circa 1970. Courtesy Gwen MacKenzie.

Norwood Hotel

97 THE PARADE, NORWOOD

In 1853, when Norwood was only a small village, residents met at the Norwood Hotel to lobby for the establishment of a district council of the 'villages of Kensington & Norwood'. Their meeting was held in a seven-room one-storey hotel that was known as the Gold Diggers Arms between 1852 and 1886. John Edmunds, first publican of the nearby Vintage Shades, was the prime mover of the campaign.

Kensington and Norwood came into being on 7 July 1853 as the second municipality in South Australia. The council's first meeting was held at the Gold Diggers Arms on 1 December 1853.

This stone and brick hotel, built in 1850, and known as the Norwood Arms until 1852, was located with sheds and stables on three quarters of an acre. In 1850 Abraham Brooks, the hotel's first publican, bought six lots with buildings that had been 'lately erected' from Charles Horace Cooper for £80. Before buying the property Brooks unsuccessfuly applied for a licence at the beginning of 1850 – his application was rejected because the hotel structure was 'unfinished'. At the next sitting of the Bench of Magistrates, on 22 March, the licence was finally granted, the finished house was viewed as being much required to supply the locals, 'situated in the centre of a populous village, but where no great traffic would pass it'.

During the speculative building boom of the late 1870s and the 1880s the hotel, which was the last to be rebuilt in the district, was renamed the Norwood. It was rebuilt in 1884 to a design by architects Henderson & Marryat, and a journalist announced prophetically that 'the house is built on an extensive scale and is likely to become a landmark in Norwood'. In their history of Kensington and Norwood, Gooden and Moore wrote that the hotel was 'once generally regarded as being too elaborate, and years before its time'. Years later it is still one of the district's most conspicuous and best-known buildings, and very much a landmark.

In January 1885 publican Johann Warncken advertised that his hotel was 'replete with every comfort and offers unrivalled accommodation to visitors'.

At the time of its rebuilding, brick was just about to make a comeback after bluestone and sandstone from the Adelaide Hills had been popular for thirty years. By the 1880s stone, especially dressed stone, had become so costly that mass-produced bricks became fashionable again.

The Norwood Hotel, William Tasker publican 1927–1943. Photo courtesy of Genevieve Rumbelow

Several publicans associated with the Norwood Hotel are remembered fondly in the district, most especially the Tasker family, the Hanns, and, more recently, Jimmy Deane and the Saturno brothers. The Taskers owned and managed the hotel between July 1927 and March 1970. The first Tasker associated with the hotel was William, who began his career as bellboy at the Gresham Hotel in the city. When he was promoted to waiter, the Italian chef, Zolezzi took him under his wing. Tasker was able to supplement his thirty bob a week wages by overseeing dinners at Government House.

While working in the city, William met a 'charming, innocent barmaid' employed at the Globe Hotel in Rundle Street. She was Albertina Gramm, who was very much under the watchful eye of her guardian Mrs Weidenbach. William and Albertina courted for several years and married in 1905. William and Tina then decided to run their own hotel together with Zolezzi. First they took over the Pier Hotel at Glenelg in 1909, but the venture was not a success. Undeterred, they tried again when they were granted the licence of the Colonist, on Norwood Parade, in 1910. They ran that hotel until 1926, when they were granted the licence of the Norwood Hotel.

The hotel had just been renovated and an additional bar room had been built in the yard to cope with the football season rush. The Taskers settled in and made their mark in Norwood. When William died in October 1943, Tina continued to manage the hotel for two years until their son Clyde, fresh from the war and the RAAF, could take over from his mother.

Before long Clyde was regarded as one of the most promising and energetic young hoteliers in the trade. As wartime building restrictions were lifted and building materials became available, he renovated the hotel's saloon. To christen it, in August 1949 he threw one of the biggest parties the hotel trade had seen for many years. Everyone in the liquor industry was invited.

The Norwood Hotel beer garden, 1952. Photo courtesy of Genevieve Rumbelow

Between 1972 and 1977 the hotel was run by well-known footballer, the 1953 Magarey Medallist Jimmy Deane, who made the hotel extremely popular. It's not often you hear of a publican selling out because the trade had become too big to handle, but that's what happened to Jimmy and his wife, Colleen. Jimmy says that Colleen 'used to sit down in the cellar. She used to take the money and all day, that's all she'd do, count the money'. So what was the secret of their success?

When he first took over, Jimmy decorated the bar with large photographic portraits of leading sportsmen. The 'Sportsman's Bar' became a huge attraction. He then established the Norwood as one of the most popular eating places in the district, with an inexpensive smorgasbord. Jimmy and Colleen easily coped with the smorgasbord and the new fish restaurant but then they leased the Golden Fleece garage next door as a bottle shop. This new venture was helped along with a little publicity.

Following the philosophy that 'it pays to advertise', Jimmy set about making his own television commercial, which went to air completely unrehearsed. To this day his family cringes with embarrassment. It was rated the worst commercial of the year, along with one of the most hated, the one that begins, 'Where do you get it?' But Deane's commercial was extraordinarily successful and 'added about 500 per cent to the trade overnight'.

The staff of the hotel also contributed to its popularity, from its cleaner, Molly, to its 'New Australian' waiter who, dressed in tails and bow tie, once tipped a full tray of beer over the mayor's wife at the opening of the short-lived fish restaurant. There were also the hotel's larger-than-life barmaids, glamorously frocked in long dresses, wigs and false eye-lashes. But the Norwood's biggest drawcard was the immensely popular chef, Mike Hastings. At a quarter to twelve each day there were long queues of customers eager to give him not only their menu choices but also their racing preferences. As for this side of the hotel's trade, Jimmy admits that under the liquor legislation, the Norwood Hotel was no more than a 'common gaming house'. The betting service came to an abrupt end when police, disguised as painters and decorators coming in for a quick bite, were also in the 'luncheon' queue.

Despite Jimmy's close brush with the law in which he nearly lost his licence, he said that if he had his life again he'd still be a publican, except he'd have a manager, then he wouldn't have to sell out when business became too big.

After Jimmy and Colleen sold the Norwood Hotel it became even more successful under its present entrepreneurial owners Leon and Adrian

Saturno, well-known for establishing the Booze Brothers outlets. Much inspired by their late father, Peter, they keep up with trends in the food, drink and entertainment industry by travelling around Australia to see what is happening elsewhere. Constantly setting the pace in the South Australian hotel industry, they opened South Australia's first 'pokie parlour' and have revamped their dining facilities several times. Holding over a thousand stock lines in red wine alone at their drive-in outlet at the Norwood Hotel, they claim to stock 4000 lines altogether, which is considerably more than the 200 they started off with when they first took over the hotel in 1977.

Osmonds Hotel of Norwood

(FORMERLY THE ORIENTAL HOTEL)

☚ 120 MAGILL ROAD, NORWOOD ☛

This was one of the last hotels to be established in the Kensington, Norwood and Kent Town area, having opened in July 1880. It was designed by architect James Cumming for brewers Beaglehole and Johnston – Cumming also designed the Old Lion Hotel in North Adelaide and the Union Hotel in Waymouth Street, Adelaide. The once beautiful exterior of the Oriental was given the 'austere' look in the 1930s, although it retained the first floor balcony overlooking Osmond Terrace for several years after that.

John Philip Lee, a former publican of the Old Lion Hotel in North Adelaide who applied for a licence four times before he was successful in establishing the Oriental, was very lucky to secure a licence at all. From the late 1870s onwards, the Licensing Bench had become increasingly cautious about granting any new licences for hotels in the inner suburbs. Its reasons for refusals included that an area was 'thickly populated', that nearby publicans objected to the extra competition, or that new hotels were viewed as simply not required. In 1883 several attempts were made by hopeful publicans wanting to establish new hotels in Norwood, Kensington and Maylands but all had their applications knocked back. After the opening of the Oriental Hotel, only the nearby Maylands Hotel was, after several attempts, granted a licence.

Lee must have been much relieved when he was able to advertise in

Alice Ryan's Oriental Hotel, circa 1910. Photo courtesy of Wally Hodgens

July 1880 the opening of the 'new and commodious hotel which is beautifully situated combining every convenience requisite for visitors desirous of obtaining a healthy suburban residence'. This commodious hotel has attracted several female publicans throughout its history, including Mary Clancey, affectionately called 'Mum' by all her customers.

Retaining the licence through a depression, a war and the progressive sixties – a total of forty-six years – Mary Clancey became a 'grand old lady', not easily forgotten. This was partly because she was always handsomely frocked, but was due more to her impressively large size and height, set off by her fair hair and blue eyes.

The reputation of a hotel is determined by its publican, and Mary Clancey certainly worked for hers. Widowed early in her marriage and left to raise three small children, she appointed her son Joe as her business partner as soon as he was old enough. It was a role he fulfilled until her death in February 1971.

Once known for its 'great sense of elegance', the hotel's front bar facing Magill Road was noted for its large scallop-shaped mirrors etched with caricatured horseracing scenes, which still survive. The Oriental was always filled with fresh flowers that Mary bought every week from the Central Market. She and her daughter Dorothy arranged the many vases of flowers every Sunday morning, and then set them in the main public rooms. Even the passage, which was used as a quiet bar where friends could talk, was decorated with fresh blooms.

Although most hotels until the late 1960s were male domains, the Oriental had a small ladies' lounge facing Osmond Terrace. It was fitted up with three or four tables, and here Mary Clancey's female customers would socialise. It was also where her friends met and, when the trade was quiet, she would join them.

Apart from becoming a dedicated churchwoman, Mary Clancey also found time to become a lover of horseracing. She would meet up with all her friends in full regalia of hat, gloves and handbag. Back at her 'homely' hotel, her interest in racing continued. Mary's illegal bookie and 'nit-keeper' were never caught by the police, despite regular lightning raids.

Her son-in-law told of the many close shaves they had before the Second World War. Detectives often turned up in disguise – perhaps tennis togs complete with racquets. But the 'nit-keeper', who always casually hung about the front door on race days, never failed to spot them. Upon the detectives' approach, the password of 'coat' or 'billygoat' was shouted through the front door. Transactions immediately ceased, and evidence was secreted away.

The front bar of Osmonds, showing the 1920s bar mirrors, Wally Hodgens and regulars, 1998. Photographed by Trevor Fox. Kensington & Norwood Civic Collection

For those who preferred less risky sporting pursuits there was the Oriental Hotel Cricket Club. Members played other teams monthly at some designated spot in the hills. Snooker and billiards were played at the hotel, and darts outside on the back verandah. The indoor sports still continue as major activities in the hotel, now run by 'Wally' Hodgens who has been publican since June 1990.

Wally has slowly upgraded Osmonds Hotel, which was in disrepair when he took it over. His hotel, which caters for people 'pretty well across the board', attracts a strong lunchtime trade from commercial and manufacturing businesses around the Stepney area and along Magill Road. In the evenings, Osmonds' food attracts a family oriented clientele. Noticeable in Wally's trade is what he calls 'the lost generation'. He is very mindful of the missing generation – the one between his much older front bar regulars and the rest of the hotel clientele who are usually well under the age of fifty. For several years a blues club has operated at the hotel on Sundays. More recently a trio playing blues and rockabilly type music has regularly entertained in the front bar on Sundays.

Rising Sun Inn

64 BRIDGE STREET, KENSINGTON

The Rising Sun Inn has two claims to fame. Firstly, it was established in 1848 by an American negro, known as 'Black Beck'. And secondly, since its re-opening as an historic inn in 1983, it has become renowned throughout South Australia for its fine cuisine.

The original pub closed its doors in 1883, and was boarded up for many years. Almost a hundred years to the day after its closure it was renovated, re-opened and licensed as an 'historic inn'. Much of the original fabric was retained and imaginatively incorporated into the new premises. While eating and drinking in such surroundings, it is only natural that diners should want to know something about the old pub's past.

The Rising Sun Inn opened as William Beck's second pub after he relinquished the licence of the nearby Robin Hood. Beck may have set about building the Rising Sun himself. He was a bricklayer among many occupations. He bought the site for £8 in 1848, and the inn was described in 1854 by the council as a nine-room brick inn.

Beck had already seen quite a bit of South Australia and Victoria before he became a publican in Kensington. He was involved in a court case from January 1847 – he had been indicted for receiving a stolen watch – at which he revealed he was once in the service of a Dr Edward Irving in America and had travelled with him to England and then on to Greenock in Scotland. From there he had come to Australia, possibly to Portland Bay in Victoria. There he was employed by a renowned pioneering family, the Hentys. After that he went to Port Fairy for seventeen months before travelling to South Australia. He worked at Bungaree Station, which was owned by the Hawker family and married Sarah Cullen, an Irish girl from County Wicklow in August 1840.

In September 1849, not long after Beck opened the Rising Sun Inn, he pioneered the first means of public transport between Kensington and the city. A cart made a round trip from the Red Lion Hotel in Rundle Street to the Rising Sun Inn, charging sixpence one way. There was room in the cart for just six people and there was no particular route. Sometimes the journey was made via the old Maid and Magpie and sometimes by way of the Britannia. The fares were reduced once others offered competitive prices.

RISING SUN INN, BRIDGE STREET, 1996. KENSINGTON & NORWOOD CIVIC COLLECTION

When Beck died in 1853, not quite fifty years old, his wife Sarah took over the inn. After 1856 the licence was shared between Sarah and her children before it was relinquished in 1867. The new owner, brewer Edwin Smith, attempted to disguise what had been essentially a private house with a tap room, so typical of pubs built before the early 1850s. From the late 1850s until the early 1870s, hotel interiors did not generally change but the façades began to look more like those of modern pubs. This is what happened at both the Rising Sun Inn and much later the Colonist at the end of 1878. In about 1868 the Rising Sun was given a handsome bluestone façade with defined parapet and ornamental pediment.

Research by local historian, Beth Brittle reveals that after the hotel was made redundant by the showy new structure of the second Rising Sun on the corner of Bridge and High streets 'the old building was in domestic use – sometimes as a shop. In 1951 it was bought by R.P. Tilbrook. For the next twenty years the only South Australian-made motorcycles were produced here by Tilbrook.'

In the late 1970s and early 1980s there was renewed interest in Kensington as a pleasant village in which to live. This created the ideal environment for the transformation of the old Rising Sun Inn into a restaurant. The pub was renovated by architect Graham Hardy for Tony Schmidt in 1983. Rod and Jane Said bought it in 1985 and they have been 'mine hosts' ever since. The Saids are able to focus exclusively on their clientele, and Rod says this is possible only because of their dedicated chefs and staff. Full of charm and character, the restaurant has won many tourism and hospitality awards. Not only popular with a regular local clientele, the restaurant attracts many interstate and international visitors.

Robin Hood Hotel

☚ 315 PORTRUSH ROAD, NORWOOD ☛

The first Robin Hood Hotel was on the site of the present Kensington Hotel, in the village of Kensington. The Robin Hood opened there on 19 March 1846, operating under this name until 1849. That hotel was rebuilt in 1849 and renamed the Globe Hotel, which it remained until 1958 when it became the Kensington Hotel.

In December 1850 Thomas Tasker applied for a licence for the Robin Hood Hotel, to be located at the present Portrush Road site, but he was initially rejected. His application before the Licensing Bench coincided with William Powell's for the Freemasons' on Wellington Street. At the hearing Tasker was described as a 'trafficker in licenses', for he had just sold his interest in the hotel that was, until 1849, known as the Robin Hood. The Justices of the Licensing Bench further said that 'Tasker sold his house and good will, and it was therefore a breach of faith for him to attempt to open another in the neighbourhood'.

Soon after its establishment on Portrush Road, Norwood in March 1851, the new Robin Hood Hotel became a popular venue for parties, fêtes, meetings, weddings and dinners. The newly formed Kensington and Norwood Council had its second meeting there, and organisations such as the Kensington and Norwood Company of Volunteers regularly met at the Robin Hood in the mid-1850s. A German Brass Band was hired to entertain the volunteers at a dinner held to mark the beginning of their military vacation in August 1855. During the toasts it was stated that these men were the 'gallant defenders of the hearth who always mustered the best, the first

Portrush Road in the 1950s. Photo courtesy of The South Australian Brewing Company

company in the colony to have arms, first to having clothing, first to have cartridges and the most complete of the force'.

Close to the hotel lived Caroline Clarke, who wrote of a wedding she witnessed in the grounds. It was a mass wedding, which even these days is an unusual event. Looking through her garden fence Caroline saw 'a dozen brides and bridegrooms assembled there for a wedding breakfast with their friends'. She wrote that 'the men generally had a white ribbon four or five inches wide tied onto the waist and over one shoulder and the horses [were] similarly ornamented round their necks'.

Between 1839 and 1908 hotels were required by law to receive the corpses of those suspected to have died unnaturally within the area. This was how the Robin Hood Hotel came to be the setting for an inquest into a suspected infanticide case in October 1851. When a female infant was found murdered she was believed to have been recently born to Jane Cardion, who was accused of the crime. But the inquest found that there was not enough evidence to support the allegations and Cardion was acquitted. The inquest decided that this was a case of 'wilful murder by persons unknown'.

The hotel was rebuilt in early 1883 during South Australia's speculative boom. After its completion to a design by Thomas English and George Soward, an advertisement appeared in the *Licensed Victuallers' Gazette* on

12 May proclaiming that 'the above well-known suburban landmark has been entirely rebuilt and now offers the best accommodation procurable in the colony. The situation is healthy, and means of ingress and egress to town most frequent by tramcars or bus. All drinks of the rarest quality. Choice cigars'.

A few years later, in 1890, the hotel was described in a gazetteer-like publication known as *Descriptive Adelaide* as being 'constructed of stone and consists of 8 bedrooms, 3 parlors (one up and 2 downstairs) large bar and bagatelle room and fitted throughout with all modern appliances for comfort and convenience . . . there is also a beautiful verandah which adds much to the attractiveness of the house'.

For much of the twentieth century the hotel was run by licensee Anna Davis. In 1955 when she was eighty-four years old, Anna was described by the *Licensed Victuallers' Gazette* as 'that grand old personality in our industry'. Davis held the licence for forty-three years from September 1914. Her son Ted had the licence from June 1957 until October 1964.

In recent times, the hotel's stables have been imaginatively renovated to create a popular courtyard restaurant. The Binns family have been mine hosts of the hotel since early 1996. Sue Binns, speaking for herself and her husband Chris and son Matthew, says that, 'Food is very big in the Robin Hood . . . hospitality is our business, and we really do try to make people feel at home in a friendly atmosphere.' The Robin Hood also has a front bar that is still very important for old-time regulars and for a lot of young people too. Adamant that the young people matter, the Robin Hood has sponsored many sporting clubs. Sue says this is all part and parcel of running a hotel. The investment is good for business and the clubs that have benefited often make the Robin Hood their meeting point.

Robin Hood is depicted in the stained glass window. Photographed by Trevor Fox. Kensington & Norwood Civic Collection

Royal Hotel

2 NORTH TERRACE, KENT TOWN

When the Royal Hotel was opened for business in early 1878 an advertisement announced that a 'new and commodious tavern has been opened by Mr J. Williams. It contains 24 convenient apartments, ten are ample domestic offices, bath rooms ... a 6 stall stable is attached to premises, a billiard room is also open in connection with the establishment which is delightfully situated opposite Bailey's Garden'.

The Royal, which is on the boundary of the city and two suburbs, was built for brewer, Edwin Smith. He bought the land in 1873. Smith was an astute businessman with a knack for recognising sites for hotels. He took particular note of what might pass close by the site at some future date. As it happened, the horse trams to Paradise passed its doors from 1883.

The Royal is similar in style to the King's Head in King William Street in the city of Adelaide which was designed by architect Thomas English. The Royal is in the Italianate design of bluestone with stucco detailing and a cantilevered balcony. Like the Britannia Hotel, it is an important landmark in the city of Kensington and Norwood. The hotel is complemented by the other two corner buildings of Yarrabee House and the impressive Romilly House, which was built as Vaughan House at the same time as the Royal. Part of Vaughan House was initially used as a first-class lodging house, and it is likely that many of its tenants were regulars at the Royal.

The hotel was for many years the local pub for employees at the old waterworks in the parklands opposite. It was also popular with the 'trammies' at the former Hackney tram depot, and workers from the Kent Town Maltings and the Rosella factory. It was also the haunt of estate agents with offices nearby and who drew up many a contract in the lounge and

The Royal Hotel about the time of its completion in 1878. SLSA: MLSA B10601

saloon bars. The Royal was also the local for many post-war Italian migrants who lived near St Peter's College. It was these groups of customers the hotel was serving when Dick Barratt took over in February 1957. He was in charge until August 1962.

A fourth generation publican, whose forebears first began trading in the 1860s, Dick had once been a well-known baritone singer in the children's choir known as 'Kangaroos on Parade'. He also had guest spots on 5AD radio in 1937 when he was about seventeen. The choir went on tour to country towns around the state raising money for charities. Young Dick Barratt was often invited to perform in concerts and to sing cowboy and popular songs earning as much as six guineas a week. His father thought it was disgraceful that a mere youth could earn such a huge sum when his own head barman at the Norfolk Hotel in the city of Adelaide was only earning £3/15/- a week. Barratt's singing career was cut short when his parents moved from the city to Port Elliot to take over the Royal Family Hotel. Before he joined the army during the war, Barratt worked for his uncle, Jean 'Belgium Joe' Mathot, who was publican at the Alma Hotel for most of the war years.

Barratt ran the Cradock Hotel, north of Orroroo, after the war, followed by a stint at the Clare Castle in Kapunda. He was then invited by one of Adelaide's most famous hoteliers, Max Flannagan, to run the Royal Hotel. Flannagan told him, 'You run it as your own pub, all I want is results.' As Dick says,'Well I was there five years and gave him results.' The Royal Hotel was not much different to any other hotel in that era, but some comments from Dick give an insight into the general daily business of a suburban hotel.

His steady trade was beautifully organised because employees at the waterworks and the 'trammies' from the Hackney depot were paid fortnightly on alternate weeks. 'When one lot were going broke, the other lot were coming good.' The Royal was always a busy pub during the six o'clock closing days. It started to fill at four o'clock and by five o'clock 'you'd be flat to the board ... with customers four deep round the big circular bar, screaming for pints'.

Dick had such a good reputation with the Norwood police that they generally phoned first before a visit and if they did make a raid it was never on race days. The police even left the hotel's bookie alone. He was 'a man about the town' who operated so discreetly that he didn't need a lookout. The bookie once confided in Dick that he was left alone because 'I always go to the taxation department to tell them what I've won and what I've lost, for if I pay my tax, they don't tell the police.'

Barratt's hotel was one of the first outside the city to serve counter meals after the war. After the Rosella factory had moved from the district in about 1961, taking valuable hotel customers with it, Barratt introduced simple meals to woo customers. His curry and rice, or mutton and two vegetables were instant hits at their cheap prices. Yet it is not strictly correct to call them counter meals because by law they could not be served at the bar counter, nor could a lounge waitress bring them to the front bar. Meals had to be served in a dining room.

As business grew, it became tiresome sending customers down to the kitchen to order their meals and then back to pick them up. To speed up the process, the lounge waitresses began bringing meals into the bar. This immediately broke two laws and prompted another Norwood publican, who was visiting the hotel at the time, to dob Dick Barratt in.

Barratt noticed that the Italian men would not shout each other drinks but instead would 'pull out a little purse and they'd put over their money, each one'. The men were easy to get on with, but kept to themselves. They never over-imbibed.

Dick Barratt, publican of the Royal Hotel, circa 1960. Photo courtesy of Richard Barratt

Dick Barratt also mentioned the wives of the Italian immigrants who lived near St Peter's College and were regular customers at the bottle shop, but never came into the hotel. It seems that Dick had a part to play in the transformation of one of the Italian women who was eager to be more 'Australian'. She was dressed, like many Italian women migrants, all in black: black stockings, shoes and headdress. She would come into the bottle shop to buy a bottle of Marsala, and she sought Barratt's advice on her appearance. He told her she would look better wearing something colourful, and that a new hairdo might not be bad either. Some time later her husband came in and asked, 'What you doing that for? Now I can't keep her home.'

For most of its history the Royal has been a busy hotel but never more than today. Under the management of Nick Grandioso, Eddie Tunbridge and Ian Steele since August 1991, the Royal Hotel has been the young people's choice in the district for late night entertainment. Taking advantage of the 1991 closing time of 4 am, the energetic partners have transformed their pub from an old traditional hotel to a complex that provides three forms of entertainment on any given night – simultaneously. Catering for different musical tastes, the hotel has a young clientele that is drawn predominantly from the eastern suburbs.

As well as the link the Royal Hotel has had for many years with the St Peter's Old Collegians, the licensees give regular sponsorship to several other collegian associations.

Apart from late night entertainment, the Royal's other thriving trade is the lunchtime business from workers in the small to medium businesses that are so much a part of Kent Town.

PART THREE

THE LOST HOTELS

Catherine Wheel

CORNER OF NORWOOD PARADE BRIDGE STREET AND HILL STREET, KENSINGTON

A licence for this hotel was first granted in August 1842. Owner John Wheland, a city publican, should have been wary – 1842 was not a good year for new licences as the new colony was experiencing its first economic recession.

Later, when he tried to sell the hotel in November 1844, there were no buyers, even though it was described by the *South Australian Register* as the 'best village inn in the province', and 'the only licensed house in the ... rising village'. It closed as a hotel in 1846, and remained unsold until May 1849 when one of Wheland's former publicans, storekeeper Edward Drew, bought it for a mere £14.

Absolute Sale.

Best Village Inn in the Province. "Catharine Wheel," Kensington.

JOHN BENTHAM NEALES, is instructed to sell THIS DAY (Saturday), the only licensed house in the above rising village, now let to a good tenant, who will remain or leave at Christmas, at the option of the

LUCKY PURCHASER.

SALE NOTICE. *SOUTH AUSTRALIAN REGISTER* 9 NOVEMBER 1844

John Wheland (sometimes spelt Whelan) was also the first publican of the Tasmanian Hotel in Hindley Street. The pub was established in 1839 and was known from 1853 until 1921 as the Adelaide Hotel. It was one of Adelaide's oldest pubs when it lost its licence in a Local Option Poll in 1921. According to Bob Hoad's *Hotels and Publicans*, Wheland was publican at the Tasmanian Hotel between 1839 and 1842, and again between 1844 and 1845. In between these two dates Wheland lived in Kensington next-door to the Catherine Wheel on Lots 100, 105 and 106. The Wheland family have been involved in South Australian pubs since settlement.

Nothing of the Catherine Wheel remains and the Kensington Centre on Norwood Parade now occupies the site.

Family Hotel

CORNER OF GEORGE STREET AND WILLIAM STREET, NORWOOD

The Family Hotel was first licensed in December 1858 as the Coach and Horses, a name it retained until 1863. It did not trade as a hotel at all after 1864 until John Crampton bought it at the end of 1868 and it was relicensed to become Crampton's Family Hotel. This name was kept until 1880, when it became simply the Family Hotel.

The former Family Hotel, George Street Norwood, 1998
Photographed by Trevor Fox.
Kensington & Norwood Civic Collection

In March 1880, the publican Mary Pearce was taken to court for suspected adulteration of the brandy she had bought from Adelaide's Milne & Son, brandy makers. The charges were dropped when it was revealed that the adulterating substance was fusel oil, then a normal additive to brandy that only became 'injurious' if drunk before the brandy was five years old. In 1909 this pretty little pub lost its licence in the Local Option Polls along with four other hotels in the district. The Family Hotel has been a private dwelling ever since.

A conveyance for June 1857 reveals that Thomas English and his partner and brother-in-law Henry Brown bought the land at what appears to be ten shillings – a give-away price. They built the hotel structure and sold it in March 1859 to Henry Johnson. On the same day of sale Johnson borrowed £600, presumably to buy the hotel.

The Family Hotel was one of Thomas English's first efforts as a hotel designer. He started working as a builder after his arrival in the colony from England in 1850, and went on to become Mayor of Adelaide in 1862 and Commissioner of Public Works between 1865 and 1867 when he was a Member of the Legislative Council. After practising architecture with Rowland Rees, he went into partnership with George Klewitz Soward until his death in 1884.

Freemasons'

19 WELLINGTON STREET, KENSINGTON

The Freemasons' operated briefly from 12 December 1850 until mid-1851, when the nearby Robin Hood Hotel put it out of business. The Wellington Street building has all the hallmarks of an early pub, hidden behind verandahs and plaster that have been added more recently.

As an early public house, built like a private dwelling, it easily became a private residence when trade fell away. At about the time that the hotel went out of business the Licensing Bench had held a meeting, in June 1851, to address the problem of poorly built hotels. The Freemasons' may have been on their agenda.

The building may have existed in 1850 because Richard Stevens secured a mortgage of £200 on his 'messuages erections and buildings'. These were to become the Freemasons' at the end of the year when he leased it to William Powell. Applications for two hotels, Thomas Tasker's Robin Hood and William Powell's Freemasons', were dealt with together at a Licensing Bench hearing on 11 December 1850. The Freemasons' was described as a 'low ill-constructed building'. It contained sixteen good-sized rooms. People expected the application to be successful because Kensington had become a busy place which carts ran to and from every half an hour. The road it was said, 'more resembled the Port Road than any other place'. A memorandum in support of the new hotel was produced showing signatures by Mr Roberts, Mr Nicholls, Mr Thornton and other residents.

William Powell was granted a licence, Thomas Tasker's application was rejected. He applied again in March 1851 and was successful. This spelled disaster for the Freemasons'.

Although official records indicate that the Freemasons' operated as a pub for only a matter of months, there is local speculation that some time before 1850 it was a sly grog outlet. Three different publicans owned the property between 1840 and 1850 and there is reference by local historian, Jim Warburton, to a grog shanty in Kensington that existed around Christmas of 1840, but it is unclear exactly where it was located.

After the pub ceased trading it became a private house. It was bought by Mortimer Burman in October 1853 for £300. Burman gave his occupation as carpenter and omnibus proprietor but he was later publican at the Robin Hood Hotel in 1864–65 and in 1870. After his death his descendants owned the property until 1967.

Artist James Shaw, known for his paintings of private houses, lived at this property for a time. He and Mortimer Burman travelled to the colony's south-east where Shaw painted the *Admella*, a ship that was wrecked in 1859. He gave the painting to Mortimer Burman, and it is now in the Art Gallery of South Australia.

The old pub is still a private residence. It is the only surviving building in the district that demonstrates how the earliest pubs looked more like private houses than public ones.

The former Freemasons',1998. Photographed by Trevor Fox.
Kensington & Norwood Civic Collection

Kensington Hotel

52-58 SHIPSTERS ROAD, BOUNDARY OF BURNSIDE AND ☚ KENSINGTON ☛

It would be easy to pass a group of one-storey houses on Shipsters Road and never know it was once a thriving pub. From 1881 until it lost its licence during the Local Option Poll of 1909, a hotel was located here opposite the tram depot and facing a large tram-turning site. Sometimes it was unofficially referred to as the Tram Terminus Hotel. Its official name was the Kensington Hotel.

It must not be confused with the present Kensington Hotel in Regent Street, which was known as the Globe Hotel throughout the trading period of the first Kensington Hotel.

This humble local was established by Richard Vaughan, owner of the East End Market. He was also known for the construction of the beautiful Botanic Hotel on North Terrace opposite the Botanic Gardens. Although on the boundary of the Burnside district, the Kensington Hotel was very much part of the village life of Kensington. Richard Vaughan owned it for only two years before transferring ownership to his brother, Alfred, who in 1894, during the economic recession, lost it to an overseas owner because of a foreclosure.

The area around the hotel was subdivided in 1876 when there was an explosion of suburban growth close to the city. Shortly after, the first horse tram was proposed to run between the city and Kensington and the plan was for the hotel to face the tram depot. It was an opportunity to cash in, but obtaining a licence for a hotel in the suburbs was becoming increasingly difficult and several attempts were necessary. An application for a hotel, to be called the Terminus Hotel, was first submitted in 1878, but when it was not built within the required six months, the land and plans were transferred to Richard Vaughan. He built the hotel and changed the name of the proposed hostelry to the Kensington Hotel. By this time the Marryatville Hotel had been relocated from its earlier site on Kensington Road to its present position on High Street and Kensington Road, and it was in the process of being rebuilt.

Apart from this competition, there were further objections from the publican at the Globe Hotel in Regent Street who was still trading from a building constructed about 1849. It is not certain how Vaughan was able to convince the Licensing Bench of the need for another hotel when there were two others in such close proximity but he was finally granted a licence in December 1880. He said that his hotel would contain thirty rooms and have first-class accommodation. Perhaps the Bench was influenced by the impressive architecture of his three-storey Botanic Hotel but the new hotel was never as grand as the Botanic. *The Licensed Victuallers' Gazette* referred to Vaughan's Kensington Hotel as 'an elegant pretentious looking, and commodious hotel' when it was first built in 1881. Alongside the hotel, Vaughan built a 'series of charmingly sited bowers done in trellis work, an institution of the continental tea gardens. Altogether the Kensington Hotel and gardens look fair to become a popular resort'.

In February 1884 Vaughan sublet his hotel to Ernest Herbert Eisfelder, who had come from the Sir James Fergusson Hotel at Tarlee in the mid-north. Although genial and affable, Eisfelder had little time for 'fanatics', especially those from the temperance fraternity. Only a few months after settling into his suburban pub he received a letter that said:

'To the Landlord of the Kensington Hotel, Sir, Please take notice that if I should at any time from this date call at your house you are NOT to provide me with liquor of any kind. Should you do so I shall prosecute you.'

It didn't take Eisfelder long to discover that 'this miserable being' was a 'red-hot Blue Ribbon Army man'. He sent the threatening letter to the Licensed Victuallers' Association for publication.

Less than a year later, on 9 June 1885, Eisfelder committed suicide by hanging himself from a hat peg behind his bedroom door. An inquest was held at the pub the day after the tragedy. It was learned that Eisfelder had become very despondent about a debt of about £2300, which he blamed on the previous licensee C. Biggins.

Eisfelder felt that Biggins had 'grossly deceived him as to the value of the hotel and the trade done in it' when he first took over the licence and Biggins claimed that Eisfelder had often threatened to shoot him. In an effort to cut his losses, Eisfelder had offered to sell the lease and the goodwill of the house for £500 to his supplier, William Wicksteed. Although Wicksteed could not give an immediate answer, he had told Eisfelder that he would call in a few days and let him know how he could help him. But Eisfelder had taken his life before Wicksteed returned.

Over the next twenty-three years until it lost its licence in 1909, the Kensington Hotel had more than twenty publicans, including twelve in eight years. This probably suggests it was a difficult hotel from which to make a living.

This building was once the Kensington Hotel, 1998. Photographed by Trevor Fox.
Kensington & Norwood Civic Collection

Kentish Arms

43 THE PARADE WEST, KENT TOWN

Nothing remains of the original Kentish Arms which was located near the rear entrance to the grounds of Prince Alfred College on the western side of Pirie Street where it meets the Parade West. The hotel lost its licence in the 1909 Local Option Polls when ratepayers voted to do away with one of their pubs. It was demolished in 1918 by C.T. Cocks to make more room for his dry-cleaning business.

His brick building now houses several small businesses. The single-storey hotel was licensed in 1856 in the name of German blacksmith Gerdt Leopoldt. It was the first hotel in Kent Town. His hotel was described in the annual rate assessments of 1859 as a six-room public house with bar and paling stable.

The Kentish Arms before being remodelled, 1865. Kensington & Norwood Civic Collection

The Kentish Arms was located a few streets from its main rival, the Kent Town Hotel. Trade may have also been upset when the Royal Hotel opened in February 1878. The Kentish Arms was 'improved' in late 1879 by the addition of a second storey and an unusual roof with dormer windows. This remodelling, which cost about £1000, was to a design by architects Campbell & Hamilton. Shortly after, the Kent Town Hotel was rebuilt.

The Local Option Polls of 1909 saw the loss of hotels that had the worst reputations, were the least viable, or were in antiquated buildings. The Kentish Arms couldn't compete with the showy architecture of the Kent Town and the Royal hotels and lost its licence.

The fact that the hotel's last two publicans were women may not have helped its chances of winning back its licence. Four of the five hotel licences lost in this poll were held by women. Mrs F.E. Millar had just taken over the Kentish Arms' licence from Western Australian publican, Lavinia Tate, who had been under official scrutiny during her brief period at the Kentish Arms in 1908.

The Licensing Court appears to have suspected Tate was 'living in sin' with her barman. The court saw such arrangements as harmful to the trade. The Licensed Victuallers' Association believed women publicans were generally losing popularity at the turn of the century. Even the president of the association had publicly announced that women were 'tending to bring the trade into disrepute . . .'

The police made discreet enquiries across the state in search of evidence but they found little to support such claims. Undeterred, the association suggested that, 'searching enquiries be made as to a prospective woman publican's respectability and the manner in which she has conducted her house if she has previously held a license'.

Lavinia Tate was subjected to searching enquiries when she was licensee of the Kentish Arms. She had been a publican in Western Australia for some years, holding licences at the Sandringham and Oceanic hotels in Perth. However, with a failing hotel business and a failed marriage, she and her son decided to try their luck in South Australia. Her former barman coincidentally travelled on the same ship to Adelaide at Christmas time in 1907. This coincidence did little to avert suspicions about their relationship. In the eyes of the liquor trade, she was now technically a 'single' woman. This pertinent fact was much discussed by the Licensing Bench, who were very keen to prevent single female publicans (including divorced or separated women) from holding licences, especially if it could be proved that their private life was 'questionable'.

The hotel after remodelling, 1879. Kensington & Norwood Civic Collection

During the licensing hearing, many witnesses were called, including the barman and Lavinia's son. Despite the investigation and searching questions, no proof was adduced to support allegations of a doubtful reputation, and Tate retained her licence.

Rising Sun Hotel

CORNER OF HIGH STREET AND BRIDGE STREET, KENSINGTON

This hotel lost its licence in 1909 and has been used since as either a boarding house or a dwelling for communal living. Its present owner, Colin Bond, well-known for his campaign for recognition of the City of Adelaide's heritage in the 1970s and 1980s, and co-author of *Preserving Historic Adelaide*, has spent many years renovating the old pub inside and out. The hotel was built to take over from the first Rising Sun Inn. The earlier inn, only a hundred yards along Bridge Street, was re-opened in 1983 as an historic inn.

The second Rising Sun Hotel was built in 1882 for Edwin Smith and operated for only twenty-six years. It was built during the speculative boom of the late nineteenth century as a showy new complex that incorporated three shops. Verandahs around the ground floor and its frontages on the corner of Kensington's two premier streets made it a prominent building in the district. It was designed in late 1881 by William McMinn as a thirty-four room hotel and the building contractor was James Shaw, who was well known for several large city projects.

McMinn was architect for several buildings, including the governor's residence at Marble Hill and the Crown & Sceptre Hotel in the city. He was also given all the credit for the design of the Mitchell Building at the University of Adelaide, although he was not entitled to it. He plagiarised the plans of

Melbourne architect Michael Egan. When Egan's plans were not implemented, McMinn drew up a variation of the plans and created a smaller scale version.

Publican Henry Newlyn, who had been at the first Rising Sun since December 1881, stayed to take over the new premises. But by February 1885 he had relinquished the licence. After he left, no publican stayed much longer than a year. For some reason the hotel was not popular with publicans, and the licence changed hands twenty-two times in twenty-six years of trading. Its failure may have been due to competition from other nearby hotels.

One publican lasted only a few weeks. Louis Augustav Rothenberg hanged himself in the passage at the foot of the stairs on 10 November 1893. He had been publican of the Hindmarsh Hotel in Adelaide between 1889 and 1893, and before that at the Waterfall Gully Hotel. Whatever problems the Rising Sun may have brought him, he brought more serious ones with him. He was a chronic alcoholic, who was about to be institutionalised at Hope Lodge at Belair. Filled with remorse and 'very much cut up' when his racehorse Duststorm was killed during a Tattersalls race, Rothenberg took his own life.

The Rising Sun shortly after completion, circa 1883. SLSA: MLSA B9721

Vintage Shades

59-61A WILLIAM STREET, NORWOOD

The Vintage Shades' first owner and publican, Joseph Edmunds, had the interests of Norwood and Kensington at heart. He was a prime mover in setting up the municipality that was formed in July 1853. When it looked likely that the district would be included in the East Torrens Council District he strove to keep Kensington and Norwood separate. According to his obituary in the *Observer*, Edmunds was one of the first to buy land in the newly subdivided township of Norwood. The virgin scrub was so dense 'it was no uncommon thing for his wife to light a bush fire to guide him to his abode, near the Vintage Shades'.

Edmunds was a London tailor from Jermyn Street. After arriving in Adelaide on the ship *Surrey* in 1838, he established a general grocery in Rundle Street, occasionally advertising in the newspapers. He then moved to Burnside to take up farming. Finally settling in Norwood, he worked in turn as tailor, winemaker, distiller and beekeeper. He became publican of his own public house in 1859 and remained so for almost three years before subleasing it to a series of others. The one-storey, nine-room Vintage Shades operated on the corner of Elizabeth and William streets and was part of a property on seven and a half acres that had a distillery, wine vaults, a vineyard, a bonded store and a villa.

After unusual events in 1859 and 1860, the distillery was closed down in favour of the public house. It seems that under the Victuallers' Licensing Act, a distiller could not hold a publican's licence, while a publican could hold a distilling licence under the provisions of the Distillation Act. By trying to obtain a satisfactory ruling on this anomaly, Edmunds more or less dobbed himself in and attracted trouble from customs, police and the Licensing Victuallers' Court.

The issue came to a head when Captain Bloomfield Douglas, Collector of Customs and Inspector of Distilleries, who was inspecting all the distilleries for a report to the Treasury, stumbled across Edmunds' distillery.

At the time of Douglas' inspection, Edmunds had not actually sold any brandy, as he was still in the distilling phase. No action could be taken because he had broken no law, if in fact there was a law to be broken. But if he sold a bottle of brandy perhaps he would be acting illegally. A ruling had to be made by one authority or another. Edmunds and Douglas conspired to bring the matter to a crisis by allowing a bottle of spirits to be sold by Edmunds to a man employed by Douglas.

The case was brought before the Police Court but was dismissed without establishing how the two regulations could work together. Douglas made an appeal to the Treasurer, and the case was lodged in the Local Court. Edmunds was promptly fined £10. His lawyer was not satisfied, and an

The Vintage Shades hotel, circa 1900. Kensington & Norwood Civic Collection

appeal was brought before the Supreme Court and adjourned. Edmunds' lawyer could not appear on the due date and the appeal was never heard. In the meantime Edmunds, who was a good-natured pillar of respectability, but now had a criminal record, locked up the worm of his distillery and petitioned the government. This led to a parliamentary select inquiry. Edmunds was exonerated, and his legal costs of about £33 were paid, but the inquiry did not untie the legal knots in the issue. Setting up the distillery had cost Edmunds £2000, and he only ever sold one bottle of spirits. An expensive bottle.

In 1875 Edmunds subdivided his property into thirty odd lots, and sold the hotel on a hundred-foot block to Patrick Martin in 1880. That June, Martin advertised the extensive additions and renovations he had made to the hotel. There was now 'a splendid large assembly room suitable for public meetings'.

Popular though the hotel may have been, its location in the smaller, densely populated back streets of Norwood meant it lost its licence in the 1909 Local Option Polls. At the time of the poll it was privately owned and basically a one-storey mid-nineteenth century structure despite its 1880 additions. This would have counted against it when its closest rivals had all been substantially rebuilt in the 1880s as two-storey structures.

The Vintage Shades was demolished recently and new houses were built in its place.

AUSTRALIAN WINE and BRANDY.—PERIODICAL SALES at EDMOND'S, NORWOOD WINE FACTORY and BONDED CELLAR, William street, Norwood.

The first Sale by Auction will take place May 25, in lots to suit purchasers, from a gallon to a pipe.

Holders of Wine can avail themselves of these sales by forwarding samples.

Manufacturers of Brandy can bond in the above Cellar under the regulations lately issued by the Government.

JOSEPH EDMUNDS' ADVERTISEMENT FOR HIS PREOCCUPATIONS OTHER THAN HIS PUB. *CHRONICLE* 7 MAY 1859

References

Chapter One

1 Interview with Mrs Kathleen Clancey, March 1997, Kensington & Norwood Oral History Collection
2 Interview with Donald Scott, July 1997, Kensington & Norwood Oral History Collection
3 Interview with Max Yeoman and Pat Thyer, May 1997, Kensington & Norwood Oral History Collection
4 *Observer* 18.1.1862, p 4
5 *South Australian Weekly Dispatch* 4.11.1854, p 5, *Adelaide Times* 21.10. 1854, *South Australian Register* 2.8.1855, p 2
6 *Chronicle* 7.7.1860, p 3
7 *Licensed Victuallers' Gazette* June 1960, p 40
8 *Licensed Victuallers' Gazette* 1.1.1881, p 1
9 *Advertiser* 29.5.1931, p 20
10 Interview, Macka MacKenzie, June 1997, Kensington & Norwood Oral History Collection
11 *Observer* 29.12. 1866, p 4
12 *Observer* 15.6.1850, p 3, 22.6.1850.
13 *Licensed Victuallers' Gazette* 25.5.1878, p 5
14 Mortlock Library of South Australiana, PRG 331/1, Caroline E. Clarke papers
15 Griffiths, Tom, (ed. 1988) *The Life and Adventures of Edward Snell: the illustrated diary of an artist, engineer and adventurer in the Australian colonies, 1849 to 1859.* p 104
16 *Licensed Victuallers' Gazette* 26.5.1883, p 5
17 Interview, Jimmy Deane, June 1997, Kensington & Norwood Oral History Collection
18 *Quiz* 22.1.1909

Chapter Two

1 Hoad, J.L. (Bob), *Hotels and publicans in South Australia,* 1986
2 General Registry Office, Memorial Books 9/375, 18/10/1847
3 *South Australian Register* 11.3.1863. This building may in actual fact have been on the site of the earlier 1840s Catherine Wheel Hotel.
4 Michael Ogden, The South Australian Brewing Company 2, p 29
5 *Licensed Victuallers' Gazette* 16.12.1876, 24.3.1883, p 5, 16.6.1883, p 5
6 *Licensed Victuallers' Gazette* 24.3.1883, p 5, 13.9.1884, p 5
7 *Licensed Victuallers' Gazette* 16.6.1883, p 5

Chapter Three

1 These periods are derived from my own observations.
2 *South Australian* 13.6.1851
3 *South Australian* 12.12.1850
4 English Heritage, Pubs: Understanding listing, p 4

Chapter Four

1 Hoad, J.L. (Bob) *South Australian Hotel Records prior to 12 February 1839,* p.vii.
2 *South Australian Register* 31.1.1846
3 E.J. Thomas 'History of South Australian Legislation' in *Public Service Review* 27.3.1930
4 *South Australian Register* 14 & 15 March 1849
5 E.J. Thomas, *op. cit.*
6 E.J. Thomas, *op.cit.*
7 South Australian Parliamentary Debates, 1858, col 885
8 *Observer* 25.10.1851, p 4
9 *Observer* 22.3.1856, p 4
10 *Observer* 3.6.1881
11 *Observer* 11.11.1893. p 27
12 *South Australian Register* 28.1.1907
13 *Observer* 7.2.1856, p 4 of supplement

14 *Licensed Victuallers' Gazette*, 24.4.1880, p 5
15 State Records, GRG 5/130 Kensington & Norwood Morning Books 1920–1
16 State Records, Police Dept, Police Commissioner, GRG 5/2, Dkt.255 of 1913
17 State Records, GRG 5/130 Kensington & Norwood Morning Books 1920–1
18 *Licensed Victuallers' Gazette* 22.3.1934, p 8
19 *Licensed Victuallers' Gazette* 20.3.1880, p 5

Chapter Five

1 Interview with Don Dunstan, July 1997, Kensington & Norwood Oral History Collection.
2 *South Australian Parliamentary Debates*, Legislative Council, 1908, cols. 472, 511
3 Hoad, J.L. *Hotels and publicans in South Australia* – 1836–1986
4 *Advertiser* 11.2.1959, p 4
5 *Advertiser* 26.7.1884, p 7
6 Hebe means the goddess of youth and spring, the cupbearer of Olympus, hence a waitress, a woman in her early youth.
7 *Advertiser* 14.8.1880
8 *South Australian Register* 16.9.1852
9 See Patricia Sumerling's history of the 'West End' in Dickey, B. (ed) 1992, *William Shakespeare's Adelaide*, 1860–1930
10 *Licensed Victuallers' Gazette* August 1939, p 29
11 *Advertiser*, 27.9.1894, p 6
12 *Licensed Victuallers' Gazette* February 1943 p 8. See also Diane Kirkby, *Barmaids: A History of Women's Work in Pubs.* pp.152–53, 1997
13 *Licensed Victuallers' Gazette* March 1956, p 28
14 See Osmonds Hotel (formerly the Oriental Hotel)
15 *Licensed Victuallers' Gazette* June 1942, p 1
16 *Licensed Victuallers' Gazette*, January 1951, p 4
17 Interview with Don Dunstan, Kensington & Norwood Oral History Collection
18 Interview with 'Macka' (Hugh Lloyd) MacKenzie; Kensington & Norwood Oral History Collection

Bath Hotel

Express & Telegraph 1.3.1909, p 1; Kensington & Norwood rate assessments 1854–1860; *Licensed Victuallers' Gazette* 9.12.1876, p 3, July 1936, p 19, March 1938, p 38, June 1942, p 23; *Observer*, 18.1.1862 p 4; State Records, GRG 67/24, Licensing Court, Register of new applicants; Interviews, Dennis O'Donoghue, Kevin Shannon and Pat Thyer, Kensington & Norwood Oral History Collection, Tony Franzon, unpublished notes, Kensington and Norwood Oral History Collection.

Britannia Hotel

Licensed Victuallers' Gazette 25.5.1878, p 5, 1.6.1878, p 6, 15.1.1878, p 4, March 1935, p 28, March 1941, p 7, April 1942, p 5, June 1944, p 7, February 1947, p 17; *Observer* 15.11.1851, p 5, 22 March 1856, p 4, 8.3.1879; State Records, Licensing Court, GRG 67/24, GRG 67/40, 19.8.1941, 12.6.1943, 16.6.1945; GRG 67/47 – Chief Inspector's annual reports 1918–47 for 1925; Interview with Con Angelopoulos, July 1997.

Colonist Tavern

Advertiser 16.2.1985; General Registry Office, RPA Application 16325; *Licensed Victuallers' Gazette* 29.11.1879, p 7, 1.1.1881, p 9, 22.3.1934, p 8; *South Australian Register* 8.1.1873, p 6, 2.1.1880, p 5; Interview, Don Dunstan, July 1997, Kensington & Norwood Oral History Collection; Interview of Heinz Keimeier, July 1997, Unpublished Notes, Kensington & Norwood Oral History Collection.

Kensington Hotel, Regent Street

General Registry Office Memorial Books 5/278, 9/375, 9/421, 16/258 and RPA Application 22917; G.W. Gooden and T.L. Moore, *50 Years of Kensington and Norwood*, p 217; *Licensed Victuallers' Gazette* November 1952, pp 12–18; *Observer*, 9.1.1847, 16.1.1847, 9.2.1856 suppl. 4; *South Australian* 6.8.1841; *South Australian Government Gazette* 19.3.1846; *South Australian Register* 4.4.1840, p 2, 15.5.1841, p 3. 14.3.1849, 25.1.1882, p 6 (tender notice), State Records, Supreme Court, GRG 36/1 Indictments Nos 21–24 of 1841; Tolmer, A., *Reminiscences of an adventurous and chequered career at home and at the antipodes*, 1882, Vol.1 p 152; Interviews Arthur Wilson, June 1997, Kensington & Norwood Oral History Collection; David Pink, July 1997, Unpublished Notes, Kensington & Norwood Oral History Collection.

Kent Town Hotel

Chronicle 7.7.1860, p3; Department of Patents Commonwealth of Australia, 1904, Nos. 2120–2121; Patents for Inventions, Abridgements of specifications, class 77, Patent Office, London, 1910, No. 14, 066; *Licensed Victuallers' Gazette* 3 June1882, p 5, 16 July 1934, State Records, GRG 67/47 Chief Inspector's Annual Reports, 1926 p 4; *Quiz* 24.9.1909, p 8; Interview Donald Scott, July 1997, Kensington & Norwood Oral History Collection; Interview Rick Panizza, July 1997, Unpublished Notes, Kensington & Norwood Oral History Collection.

Marryatville Hotel

Gooden, G.W. and Moore, T.L. *50 years of Kensington and Norwood*, 1903, pp 217–8; *Licensed Victuallers' Gazette* 3.2.1883, p 11, November 1959, p 36; *South Australian Register* 13.12.1880; State Records, GRG 67/40,Inspection of hotels, Dkt 187 for Marryatville Hotel, GRG67/47 Chief Inspector's Annual Reports for 1937; Interview with Mr and Mrs Max Yeoman, May 1997, Kensington & Norwood Oral History Collection.

New Alma Hotel

Chronicle 30.10.1909, p 45; *Licensed Victuallers' Gazette* 22.6.1878, p 4, 1.3.1879, p9, 10.11.1883, March 1935, p28, August 1939; *Observer* 3.6.1881; *Quiz* 5.11.1909, p 8; State Records, GRG 67/ 24 – Register of new publicans; J Statton, *Biographical index of South Australians* for T. Pegler and R. Standley, 1986; Interview (Hugh Lloyd) MacKenzie, Alan Brennan, Clacka (Gordon) Clark, May Murdoch, Kensington & Norwood Oral History Collection; Ian Menzies, unrecorded interview, unpublished notes, Kensington & Norwood Oral History Collection.

Norwood Hotel

Advertiser 1.2.1959, p 4; Gooden, G.W. and Moore, T.L., *50 Years of Kensington and Norwood*, p 218; GRO Real Property Application No 20069; *Licensed Victuallers' Gazette* 6.12.1884, p 5, 17.1.1885, p 8, August 1949, p 28, November 1952, pp 12–18; *Observer* 23.3.1850 p 3, 15.6.1850, p 3, 22.6.1850, 1.9.1855, p 5; State Records, Colonial Secretary, *South Australian Gazette* 28.3.1850, p 201; *South Australian Register* 12.4.1884, p 2 (tender ntoice), 18.4.1884, p 2; State Records, GRG 24/4, Colonial Secretary, Dkt 924/1853; GRG 67/24 Register of new applicants, GRG 67/47 – Chief Inspector's annual reports 1926; Woods, J., *The Magarey Medal*, pp 161–164, 1988; Interview Colleen and Jimmy (James Grant) Deane, June 1997, Kensington & Norwood Oral History Collection; Adrian and Leon Saturno, July 1997, Unpublished Notes, Kensington & Norwood Oral History Collection.

Osmonds Hotel of Norwood

Licensed Victuallers' Gazette 3.7.1880, p 1, 24.3.1883, p 5; *South Australian Register* 1.1.1879, 11.11.1879, 2.1.1880, 28.1.1907, p 7; Interviews, Kathleen D. Clancey, March 1997 and Mr R. and Mrs D. Stentiford 9 April 1997, Kensington & Norwood Oral History Collection; Wally Hodgens, July 1997, Unpublished Notes, Kensington & Norwood Oral History Collection.

Rising Sun Inn

Observer 16.1.1847, p 6, 20.2.1847, 27.2.1847, 13.3.1847, 30.8.1851, p 5; *South Australian Register* 12.9.1849, 13.10.1853 (Beck's death notice), 22.7.1911, p 8, 29.4.1920, p 5, 23.4.1923, p 8; Rod Said, July 1997, Unpublished Notes, Kensington & Norwood Oral History Collection.

Robin Hood Hotel

Adelaide Times 21.10.1854, p 33; General Registry Office, Memorial Books 5/278, 9/375, 9/421, 16/258; *Licensed Victuallers'Gazette* 12.5.1883, p 1; Mortlock Library, PRG 331/1 Caroline Emily Clarke papers, p 152; *Observer* 25.10.1851, p 4, 29.12.1866, p4; Smillie, J., *Descriptive Australia and Federal Guide; South Australian* 12.12.1850, p 3, 14.3.1851; *South Australian Register* 2.8.1855, p 2; *South Australian Weekly Dispatch* 4.11.1854, p 5. Interview Sue Binns, July 1997, Unpublished Notes, Kensington & Norwood Oral History Collection.

Royal Hotel

Licensed Victuallers' Gazette 23.2.1878, p 6; Warburton, E., *St Peters: a suburban town*, 1983, pp 64–6; Interviews, Dick Barratt, July 1997, Kensington & Norwood Oral History Collection; Interview Nick Grandioso July 1997, Unpublished Notes, Kensington & Norwood Oral History Collection.

Catherine Wheel

General Registry Office, RPA Application 1247; Hoad, J.L. (Bob), *Hotels and Publicans, 1836–1986*; *Licensed Victuallers' Gazette* November 1952, pp 12–18; *South Australian Gazette* 18.12.1845, p 388; *South Australian Register* 10.4.1841, p 4, 13.8.1842, 9.9.1844.

Family Hotel

General Registry Office, Real Property Act Application No 9560, 18.11.1868; *Licensed Victuallers' Gazette* 20.3.1880, p 5; S. Marsden, P. Stark & P. Sumerling, *Heritage of the City of Adelaide: an illustrated guide,* 1990, pp 144, 150.

Freemasons'

GRO, RPA Application 20629; Heritage Investigations, Kensington and Norwood Heritage Survey 1985; Hoad, J.L. (Bob), *Hotels and Publicans in South Australia, 1836–1986,* pp 83, 431–2; Lands Titles Office CTs 487/135, 847/125, 1524/13; *South Australian* 12.12.1850, 14.3.1851; *South Australian Gazette* 19.12.1850; Warburton, J.W., *Five Creeks of the River Torrens.*

Kensington Hotel, Shipsters Road

Chronicle 13.6.1882, p 22; Hoad, J.L., Verbal information, 21.8.1997; *Licensed Victuallers' Gazette* 18.12.1880, 19.3.1881, p 5, 19.5.1881, p 5, 3.2.1883 (advert), p 13, 6.10.1883, p 8, 23.2.1884, p 5, 11.10.1884, 13.6.1885, p 5, 2.7.1887, p 6.

Kentish Arms

Hoad, J.L. (Bob), *Hotels and Publicans,* 1836–1986; Kensington & Norwood rate assessments; *South Australian Gazette* 11.7.1850, p 418 (naturalisation of Leopoldt); *South Australian Register* 2.1.1880, p 5; State Records, GRG 67/76 Licensing Applicants 1905–8, 10.3.1908 Lavinia Tate of Kentish Arms Hotel.

Rising Sun Hotel

Licensed Victuallers' Gazette 2.6.1882, 7.10.1882, 26.5.1883, p 5, 21.2.1885, p 5; *Observer* 11.11.1893, p 27; *South Australian Register* 31.10.1881, p 2; S. Marsden, P. Stark, & P. Sumerling, *Heritage of the City of Adelaide: an illustrated guide,* pp 266–267.

Vintage Shades

Chronicle 7.5.1859, advertisement; Kensington and Norwood Rate Assessments; *Licensed Victuallers' Gazette* 19.6.1880, p 1; *Observer* 25.10.1890, p 30, obit. of J. Edmunds; *South Australian Parliamentary Papers* No 82 of 1862, Report of the select committee ... to inquire into the allegation in the petition of Joseph Edmunds; *South Australian Register* 10.4.1841, p 1.

Bibliography

Parliamentary

Report of the select committee ... to inquire into the allegation in the petition of Joseph Edmunds, South Australian Parliamentary Papers, no.82, 1862.

South Australian Government Gazette.

South Australian Parliamentary Debates (Hansard).

South Australian Parliamentary Papers.

Newspapers and Journals

Adelaide Times

Advertiser

Chronicle

Express & Telegraph

Licensed Victuallers' and Sporting Gazette

Observer

Public Service Review

Quiz

South Australian

South Australian Register

South Australian Weekly Dispatch

Archival sources

General Registry Office, Memorial Books, Real Property Act Applications

Kensington and Norwood Civic Collection: The City of Norwood, Payneham and St Peters

State Records

GRG 5 Police Department

GRG 24 Colonial Secretary

GRG 36 Supreme Court

GRG 67 Licensing Court

Theses and other unpublished papers

Adair, Daryl *Respectable, Sober and Industrious: A Social History of Public Houses and Alcohol in Early Colonial Adelaide, 1836–c.1870.* BA Hons thesis, Flinders University of South Australia, 1989

Ogden, Michael *The South Australian Brewing Company*, 1986

Books

Blackburn, M.A. *The history of Kensington and Norwood*, 1954

Bond, Colin and Ramsay, Hamish *Preserving Historic Adelaide*, Rigby, Adelaide, 1978

Dickey, B. (ed) *William Shakespeare's Adelaide, 1860–1930*, Association of Professional Historians, 1992

Freeland, J.M. *The Australian Pub*, Sun Books, Melbourne,1977

Freeland J.M. *Architecture in Australia; a history*, Penguin Books Australia Ltd, 1982

Gibson-Wilde, Dorothy & Bruce *A pattern of pubs–Hotels of Townsville 1864–1914*, History Department, James Cook University 1988

Gooden, G.W. and Moore, T.L. *50 years of Kensington and Norwood, 1853–1903*, Wakefield Press, Adelaide, facsimile edition, 1997

Hoad, J.L. (Bob) *Hotels and publicans in South Australia 1836–1984*, Australian Hotels Association (South Australian Branch), 1986

Kirkby, Diane *Barmaids: A History of Women's Work in Pubs*, Cambridge University Press, 1997

Manning, D., and Peake, A.J. *Kensington and Norwood Sketchbook*, Rigby, Adelaide, 1976

Marsden, S., Stark, P., & Sumerling, P.J., *Heritage of the City of Adelaide: an illustrated guide*, Corporation of the City of Adelaide, 1990

Mass-Observation, *The Pub and the People: a worktown study*, The Cresset Library, London, 1987

Painter, Alison *Jolly Good Ale and Old: The history of Coopers Brewery 1862–1987*, Cooper & Son, Adelaide, 1987

Smillie, J. *Descriptive Australia and Federal Guide*, Adelaide, 1890

Statton, J. *Biographical index of South Australians*, South Australian Genealogy and Heraldry Society Inc., 1986

Sumerling, Patricia 'The West End' in Dickey, B. (ed), *William Shakespeare's Adelaide 1860–1930*, Association of Professional Historians, Adelaide, 1992

Tolmer, A. *Reminiscences of an Adventurous and Chequered Career at Home and at the Antipodes*, London, 1882

Warburton, E. *St Peters: a suburban town*, The Corporation of St. Peters, 1983

Wood, John *The history of the Magarey Medal*, published by the author, Adelaide,1988

Young, Mayse *No place for a woman – the autobiography of outback publican Mayse Young*, Pan Macmillan Publishers Australia, 1992

Monographs and pamphlets

The Adelaide Pub 1837–1900, Survey by third year architectural students of Louis Laybourne Smith School of Architecture, March 1968

English Heritage, *Pubs: Understanding listing*, 1994

McLellan, J. Adelaide's early inns and taverns, Pioneers Association of SA, 1941

Ward, Maurice H. *Some brief records of brewing in South Australia*, Pioneers Association of SA, 1950

Hotel publicans of Kensington, Norwood and Kent Town

Bath Hotel

232 The Parade (south–east corner Queen Street), Norwood

Existed 13.3.1856–1993 – ?

Known as Bath Hotel 13.3.1856–29.4.1987

Known as The Parade Tavern 30.4.1987–1993 – ?

13.3.1856 SKELTON, Henry
7.4.1864 WHITEHORN,William
11.12.1876 ALLWORDEN, Mrs Margaret von
10.9.1877 MURPHY, Michael
8.12.1879 SMITH, James
19.1.1882 MURPHY, Michael
12.5.1884 GOWNE, Edwin Dave
25.9.1886 MURPHY, Michael
4.10.1892 MURPHY, Margaret
23.11.1892 BARRETT, John R.
1896 HUBBLE, George C.
1.11.1897 FISHER, Charles
17.4.1899 HOLLAND, Thomas
17.11.1899 HOLLAND, Mrs. Catherine
10.12.1900 BAKER, Edward
1912 MORAN, M.J.
1914 BAKER, Edward
10.5.1921 BAKER, Edward & STRATTON, William
About 1921 BAKER, Edward
17.9.1926 PETTITT, M.F.H. & PETTITT, F.A.
14.1.1929 PARKER, Earl S.
1930 PARKER E.F.
14.9.1936 COATS, Britton
11.10.1937 SCOTT, Mrs Kathleen Esther & SIRES Walter Thomas
15.12.1938 COMLEY, Harold Edward
22.4.1940 WILLIS, Percival Alfred Albert
29.9.1941 KILLICOAT, Mrs Rose Adelaide
22.5.1950 FRIEBE, Lyndsay Garfield, FRIEBE, Norma Bischof & FRIEBE, Ord Ronald
1.7.1954 FRIEBE, Lyndsay Garfield, FRIEBE, Norma Bischof, FRIEBE, Ord Ronald & FRIEBE, Mavis Armistice
19.12.1955 FRIEBE, Lyndsay Garfield
16.10.1959 THYER, Lance Alvin
1.1.1967 MULCAHY, Harold & WALSH, Michael James
22.9.1967 MEWETT, Donald Leonard
20.10.1969 WALSH, Michael James
9.8.1971 SHANNON, Kevin William
24.8.1971 MEWETT, Donald Leonard
1.11.1976 PROBERT, Kym Gregory
9.1.1977 MEWETT, Donald Leonard
7.4.1977 WARD, Keith Robert
20.6.1979 POWER, Terry
20.7.1981 SCHULZE, Francis Ernest
7.3.1983 SULLIVAN, Peter John & SULLIVAN, Rita Dorothy
11.11.1985 LAPPIN, Peter Vincent
3.2.1987–93 FRANZON, George & FRANZON, Robert Vincent

Britannia Hotel

1 Kensington Road (north side, east corner Fullarton Road), Norwood

Existed 20.6.1850–1993 – ?

20.6.1850 WILLIAMS, Thomas
18.12.1851 PREST, John
20.5.1852 CLARK, Sarah
17.3.1853 LANE, John
27.10.1853 BUCKLEY, John
11.9.1856 GARLAND, William
5.4.1860 GARLAND, Ann
6.4.1865 HEED, John
1866 COOMBE, T.L.
3.10.1867 HEED, John
12.12.1870 HATHWAY, Charles
11.9.1871 GARLAND, Ann
8.3.1875 WEBER, Peter
10.6.1878 RUSBRIDGE, William
9.6.1879 RYAN, Michael
12.8.1881 RYAN, Eliza
27.7.1882 McFIE, Thomas
7. 4. 1885 McFIE, Mary
28.6.1887 AIKEN, Oliver
27.7.1899 CARR, John J.
9.9.1902 AIKEN, Oliver
1906 AIKEN, Mrs Kate
1910 LEAN, William F.G.
1913 McARTHUR, Mrs Ellen
1914 COMLEY, Herbert
30.10.1919 COMLEY, Mrs Beatrice
13.2.1927 HOCKING, William
7.7.1930 JENNINGS, Elizabeth & TRESTRAIL, Horace J.S.
20.6.1938 CAMPBELL, Mrs. Elsie Eileen
8.5.1939 GOYDER, Mrs. Florence Ivy
15.9.1941 GOYDER, Mrs Florence Ivy and SKINNER, Lloyd
29.10.1945 MADIGAN, John Laurence & BEDSON, Lindsay Neil
15.11.1948 DIGBY, Edward Victor
2.11.1952 FURNER, Francis Osmond & FURNER, Henry James
13.2.1956 THOMSON, Mrs Katie Symington
5.5.1961 THOMSON, Bruce Laidlaw
9.1.1964 NORTHCOTT, Colin Frank
2.7.1967 NORTHCOTT, Colin Frank & SMITH, Harold Kitchener
4.7.1976 SMITH, Harold Kitchener
23.2.1977 SMITH, Mark Delo
18.4.1977 SMITH, Harold Kitchener
14.5.1979 WHITTING, Robert John
10.7.1980 BROWN, Desmond Albert
11.8.1980 WHITTING, Robert John
7.6.1981 STANDING, Barry Thomas
1.4.1982 PAECH, Kym Laurence
12.11.1982 BORCHARDT, Kenneth Ronald
17.6.1983 MILES, Robert Gary
25.9.1984 BLACK, James Ernest
26.8.1986 STUART, John McDouall
28.9.1987 INGLIS, Dirk Campbell
26.10.1988 CHESSELL, Gary Ronald
11.4.1990 TARCA, Nadio Emilio
25.7.1990 STURDY, David Ross
11.9.1991 CRADDOCK, Ronald Ernest
11.10.1991 SABATINO, Mario
26.11.1991 WAITE, Alan Keith
10.2.1992 ANGELOPOULOS, Chris
16.4.1992 VAHLDIECK, Edward
28.1.1993–? ANGELOPOULOS, Chris

Catherine Wheel

Kensington

Existed 11.8.1842–March 1846.

11.8.1842	WARE, Robert
27.4.1843	ANDERSON, William
4.4.1844	PATERSON, Alexander
27.3.1845	DREW, Edwin
8.12.1845–March 1846	HESELTINE, George

The Colonist

44 The Parade (south-west corner Sydenham Road), Norwood

Existed: 3.4.1851–1993 – ?

Known as Old Colonist Inn 3.4.1851 – 11.12.1893

Known as Old Colonist Hotel 12.12.1893 – 9.7.1981

Known as The Colonist Tavern 10.7.1981 – 1993–?

3.4.1851	HOBBS, Frederick
Early 1852	? Possible cessation of trading
31.3.1853	HOBBS, Elizabeth
29.3.1855	BRISTER, James
25.3.1857	KILLICK, Tiesdell
3.4.1862	DYKE, Richard
6.4.1865	DOORNE, Henry
10.1.1867	DOORNE, Ellen
12.12.1870	JENNINGS, John
9.3.1874	TIGHE, James
13.3.1876	MILLMAN, James
8.9.1879	BORN, Frederick
29.9.1881	BROOKS, Charles Henry
2.2.1882	SORRELL, George
22.6.1886	McGOWAN, Robert
11.7.1893	TUXFORD, William
10.9.1895	RICHARDSON, Robert George
25.2.1897	BARRY, William H.
25.2.1898	POOLE, Alfred E.
9.8.1898	FOODY, John
30.6.1899	OSBORNE, Thomas R.
15.2.1901	ADDICOAT, Albert
9.9.1902	HARMER, Francis B. & MODY, Henry
9.6.1903	RICHARDSON, Robert George
17.10.1906	PINCHBECK, James
1910	TASKER, William H.
1927	VINCENT, Mrs T.J.
1930	WILLIS, F.W.
1931	SHAUGHNESSY, R.J.
22.10.1934	THOMPSON, Merton J.
1936	THOMPSON, J.
15.6.1937	CLENDINNEN, Mrs Euphemia Agnes
21.1.1942	MOORE, Mrs Euphemia Agnes [formerly CLENDINNEN]
2.11.1952	MOODY, Alexander Charles
12.11.1952	MOORE, Mrs Euphemia Agnes
16.11.1954	MOODY, Charles Henry Alexander
16.2.1955	MOORE, Mrs Euphemia Agnes
16.7.1967	HANSEN, Harold Morris
21.5.1972	QUINTRELL, William Henry, Ethel May, Gillian Elizabeth & HICKS, Marilyn Joy
2.7.1973	QUINTRELL, William Henry, Ethel May & FELT, Gillian Elizabeth [previously QUINTRELL, & HICKS, Marilyn Joy
18.8.1975	KIERNAN, Sean Patrick
22.10.1976	RANDEL, Patricia
29.7.1977	ARIS, Harry
29.3.1978	BUSS, Kevin Leonard
16.3.1979	SAWKA, Andrew
22.2.1980	MARSH, David Wayne
24.10.1980	CONSTANTINOU, Lucky Aspostolos
16.1.1983	MERCURI, Carmela Grazia
2.2.1986	DARCY, David John
5.5.1988	BRETT, Michael Eric
27.1.1989	ALI, Souham
13.12.1989	BARATH, Victor
26.3.1990–93 – ?	VENABLES, Mark Sandford

Family

William Street (north side, west corner George Street), Norwood

Existed 22.12.1858–1909

Known as Coach and Horses Inn 22.12.1858–April 1863.

Known as Crampton's Family Hotel 18.2.1869–13.6.1887

Known as Family Hotel 14.6.1887–1909

22.12.1858	JOHNSON, Henry
1.9.1859	BARNETT, John
28.4.1861–April 1863	JOHNSON, Henry
April 1863–17.2.1869	Did not trade as a hotel.
18.2.1869	CRAMPTON, John
11.3.1873	TUXFORD, John LeFevre
14.12.1874	HANN, Asher
13.3.1876	ELLERY, James A.
11.9.1876	CROUCHER, Joseph Owen
11.6.1877	BAUM, Carl Heinrich Wilhelm
1878	CRAMPTON, Annie
1878	PEARCE, Samuel
11.12.1879	PEARCE, Mary
16.12.1879	PEARCE, Samuel
24.3.1880	CRAMPTON, Annie
8.4.1880	GIDDINGS, William
4.4.1887	WHELAN, Margaret
1.10.1891	ROSSITER, Robert
8.2.1893	FIELD, Walter T.
1896	PILCHER, Charles
10.9.1897	PILCHER, James Robert
10.12.1897	HARRISON, Hilton
14.6.1898	DOLMAN, Charles
29.9.1899	WARNCKEN, Mrs Frances
10.10.1901	NEVILLE, Mrs Sabina
1905	WEBB, Jno.
1907	PINCHBECK, Charles
1909	STEPHENSON, Mrs M.R.

Freemasons'

19 Wellington Street, Kensington

Licensed only in 1850

1850	POWELL, W.

Kensington Arms

Kensington

Existed: 11.6.1840– Early 1842 [a mud hut]

11.6.1840	SCOTT, Henry
31.3.1841–Early 1842	BALL, Thomas

Kensington

23 Regent Street (north side, east corner Thornton Street), Kensington

Existed: 8.8.1849–1993 – ?

Known as Globe Inn 8.8.1849 – 2.4.1851

Known as Globe Hotel 3.4.1851 – ?

Known again as Globe Inn ? – Mar. 1876–Jun. 1878 – ?

Known again as Globe Hotel ? – 1880–13.8.1958

Known as Kensington Hotel 14.8.1958 – 1993 – ?

8.8.1849	WATSON, Henry
23.3.1854	THOMPSON, John
1.3.1855	SHAKEL, Ed.
31.3.1858	PEARCE, Walter
22.6.1858	BARNETT, Isaac Thomea
23.5.1859	McLEAN, William
3.4.1862	DEGENHARDT, August
13.3.1871	McGREGOR, Alexander
11.6.1877	GANDY, Edward Scott
10.6.1878	WHITBREAD, John James
28.1.1880	WELLS, Thomas
16.12.1880	McDONALD, Alexander
23.1.1882	SMITH, William Wilson
19.5.1888	LEAHY, James
11.7.1890	VENN, Joseph Augustus
12.3.1895	OLIFENT, William
10.3.1896	HARDIGEN, Henry J.
12.3.1912	HARDEGEN, John
10.6.1913	MORAN, Michael
9.6.1914	BAKER, Mrs Gertrude C.
24.10.1919	SHAW, Frederick A.
12.11.1921	BAKER, Mrs Gertrude C.
28.11.1921	CAMPBELL, Duncan
8.5.1923	LEAHY, Thomas
31.3.1924	TEAGUE, Mrs Amy
6.3.1939	FOX, Henry John Farmer

5.5.1951	FOX, Henry John Farmer,
	FOX, Anne Adelaide & George Henry
15.5.1961	FOX, Anne Adelaide & George Henry
30.1.1964	FOX, Anne Adelaide
1.10.1964	FOX, Anne Adelaide & Betty Florence
5.10.1969	HATHERLY, Maxwell James
3.8.1970	HATHERLY, Maxwell James &
	Juliana Katerina
11.1.1973	YOUNG, Reginald Bruce
5.2.1973	HATHERLY, Maxwell James &
	Juliana Katerina
28.5.1979	EDWARDS, John
19.10.1979	DILLON, Patrick Anthony
19.11.1979	FREEMAN, Allen
30.11.1982	BANKS, William Dudley
18.6.1984	WILSON, Keith Maxwell &
	WILSON, Verona Madge
31.8.1987	LAIDLAW, William Richard
1.5.1989–93 – ?	PINK, David Bernard Alexander

Kensington Hotel

Shipster's Road (east side, between Kensington and Park Roads) Kensington Park

Existed: 10.3.1881–1909

Lost licence following Local Option Poll

10.3.1881	VAUGHAN, Richard
24.2.1882	BULL, George
20.8.1883	BIGGINS, Charles
11.2.1884	EISFELDER, Ernest
23.6.1885	EISFELDER, Sarah
12.2.1886	SPONG, George Wingrove
9.5.1887	ROSS, Boorn
6.2.1888	STEPHENSON, Henry
14.2.1888	STEPHENSON, Sarah Jane
5.6.1888	SIMMS, Charles
2.2.1889	TILLEY, Robert
28.5.1890	KNAPP, George
16.7.1890	POMEROY, Adolphus
22.11.1890	LEAHY, William
24.4.1891	LEAHY, James
22.5.1891	JACKSON, Richard B.
4.5.1892	McGREGOR, Alexander
1896	WEIDENBACH, Benno
23.7.1897	MILLER, John
14.2.1898	DREW, Mrs Elizabeth A.
22.2.1899	HEYNEN, Mrs Mary
31.5.1901	NANKERVIS, John H.
1906	WISEMAN, Mrs
1907	ZANKER, William
1909	ZANKER, C.F.W.
1909	BLEECHMORE, Mrs Janet

Kent Town Hotel

76 Rundle Street (south side, west corner College Road), Kent Town

Existed: 13.3.1856–1993 – ?

13.3.1856	SIMS , William Henry
25.3.1857	CHITTLEBOROUGH, James
20.12.1860	SIMS, William Henry
28.3.1861	MOORE, Joseph
7.4.1864	EWART, Rownson
6.4.1865	LEAVER. William
12.9.1868	SAVAGE, William
8.9.1873	JACOBY, Daniel
9.3.1874	BORN, Thomas
18.7.1889	SIMMS, Charles
3.3.1892	PINCHBECK, Alfred
1895	OPIE, Joseph R.
3.5.1901	BERKHOLZ, Herman A.
1902	BERKHOLZ, Alex.
1904	O'HARA, Samuel
1905	CLARKE, Frederick
1913	PINCHBECK, James
1923	WHITE, William N.
1924	JOHNS, Gilbert E.
14.2.1938	COOLING, Charles Maurice
20.12.1941	COOLING, Mrs Mary Philomena
14.2.1948	CORNELIUS, Harold Reginald
	Richard
24.6.1959	CORNELIUS, Lance Finn
4.7.1960	SCOTT, Donald Thomas, Mary
	Elizabeth, & Percy Thomas
11.7.1960	SCOTT, Donald Thomas &
	Mary Elizabeth
Aug 1970	SCOTT, Donald Thomas &
	ROGERS, Mrs Mary Elizabeth
	(nee SCOTT)
24.3.1971	SCOTT, Donald Thomas
25.9.1972	CLIFFORD, John De Sales &
	CLIFFORD, Susanne Mary
15.2.1976	COCK, Danny
9.4.1976	SILLS, Peter Owen
21.6.1976	RYAN, Philip James &
	RYAN, Joan Antoinette
7.12.1979	NORIS, Claude & Maria
31.1.1982	ION, Graham Ronald
20.5.1983	SMITH, Brian John
18.2.1985	NORIS, Claude & Maria
1.12.1985	TREMAINE, Ronald John
15.10.1986	HENDERSON, James Fearon
25.4.1988	MORGAN, Steven Douglas
10.5.1988	HENDERSON, James Fearon
12.12.1989	GUN, Becki Townsend
7.5.1990	SANGSTER, Howie Gordon
22.8.1990	EYEARS, Robert
28.9.1992	JARVIS, Adam Bickford
21.12.1992–93–?	PATERSON, Colin Leslie

Kentish Arms Hotel

Kent Road (south side, east corner Young Street) [now the south east corner Grenfell Street and The Parade West], Kent Town

Existed: 1855–1909

1855	LEOPOLDT, G.
1856	BEHN, F.
1857	LEOPOLDT, G.
1865	CLANCY,G.
1865	MILES, F.J.
1866	LILLYWHITE, T.
1867	LILLYWHITE, C.R.
1867	PLOTZER, A.
1869	PLOTZER, S.
Early 1870	GERDT, L.
Sept. 1870	BARNETT, I.T.
1871	HARDY, D.
1871	WRIGHT, P.
Mid 1872	SMITH, Edwin Thomas [landlord]
9.9.1872	WRIGHT, William
11.9.1876	PINCHBECK, Mrs Sarah Painter
10.12.1877	PINCHBECK, Alfred
3.2.1882	SHARPE, James
9.1.1884	BARNETT, Samuel
3.6.1889	JAHN, Mrs Mary Ann
3.10. 1890	CANDLER, Mrs Elizabeth Frances
22.5.1891	ABERNETHY, Charles
5.4.1892	BOHM, Heinrich A.
7.11.1892	MILLER, James
11.12.1894	CLARKE, Frederick
15.3.1897	BURN, Mrs Amy
3.8.1900	PILE, Mary A.
13.12.1900	STEPHENSON, James E.
16.4.1901	BERRYMAN, Thomas
1904	BROWN, Albert Voules
1906	DELMONT, A.O.
1908	NOLAN, Ed. McM.
1909	MILLAR, Mrs F. E.

Marryatville Hotel

239 Kensington Road (north side, west corner Shipster's Road), Kensington

Not the first site – originally located on opposite side of road (corner of Kensington and Clapton Roads), transferred to present site 14.12.1880. The original location became the site for Marryatville's first Police Station.

Existed: 17.6.1857–1993 – ?

Known as Marryatville Hotel 17.6.1857–13.12.1880

Known as New Marryatville Hotel 14.12.1880–1881 – ?

Known again as Marryatville Hotel ? – 1897–1993 – ?

17.6.1857	CANTON, George
24.2.1858	TAYLOR, David
13.9.1858	FORBES, Harriet

Late 1858 TAYLOR, David

22.12.1858 CATCHLOVE, C.

31.3.1859 MARTIN, Richard

3.4.1862 PETTITT, Eliza

2.4.1863 MOREY, Benjamin

8.6.1868 COX, John

12.6.1871 HARRIS, William

13.3.1877 PINCHBECK, James

10.6.1878 CARLIER, Walter Bramier

12.7.1881 HARDING, George & HARDING, John

20.10.1881 HINCE, Mrs Rachel

7.8.1883 EDWARDS, Henry

5.5.1890 WALLIS, Charles Edwin

27.1.1894 LOGAN, James

1895 BINNIE, Robert

15.1.1901 DAVISON, Alexander

1904 COCK, Jonathon

1908 PURCHES, John

1901 ROWE, William

1914 SIGGINS, Mrs Rebecca V.

1923 PEARCE, Annie

1924 SIGGINS, Mrs Rebecca V.

1928 COMLEY, Mrs Beatrice

21.9.1935 COMLEY, Percy P.R.

15.11.1936 CAMPBELL, Elsie E.

15.7.1937 MATHOT, Jean Joseph

27.5.1940 YEOMAN, Horace Alexander

1.7.1948 YEOMAN, Horace Alexander, Maxwell Alexander, & COX, Sylvan Elleton Ordell

18.1.1950 YEOMAN, Horace Alexander & Maxwell Alexander

8.5.1955 WILLIAMS, Leonard Escourt

28.10.1977 REYNOLDS, Gordon Victor

5.10.1979 WILLIAMS, Barrie George

17.11.1980 BARRON, Keith Douglas

14.1.1983 REYNOLDS, Gordon Victor

9.5.1985 GRAY, Robert Charles

16.7.1985 PINK, David Bernard Alexander

29.6.1989 MARTIN, Michael George Allinson

30.4.1991 MORELLI, Peter John

25.3.1993–? NEAGLE, Andrew James

New Alma

66 Magill Road (south–east corner Sydenham Road)

Norwood

Existed: 21.6.1855–1993 – ?

Known as Alma Inn 21.6.1855 – March 1875

Known as Alma Hotel March 1875– 1993 – ?

21.6.1855 STANDLEY, Robert

20.3.1856 GIBBISON, James

27.9.1860 CRANSTON, Matthew

29.9.1864 WANSTALL, James

9.4.1868 THOMSON, William

8.6.1868 LOGAN, William

Early 1870 BAILEY, William & SISON, Frederick

13.6.1870 FOODY, Michael

11.9.1871 PEGLER, Thomas J.

7.11.1883 PEGLER, Mrs Elizabeth S.

1.3.1888 O'BRIEN, William

1.5.1889 O'BRIEN, Elizabeth Sarah

11.6.1895 BOTHE, Heinrich W.

10.3.1896 O'HARA, Samuel

8.9.1896 GANDY, Charles W.D.

20.1.1897 PORTER, Thomas

27.12.1900 PINE, Elizabeth

11.3.1902 CLARKE, Mrs Ellen

11.6.1912 ALLEN, Henry

11.3.1913 SPEED, Mrs Maggie S.

27.3.1916 McCAWLEY, Emily Marion

24.10.1916 AUSTIN, Joseph

19.7.1922 CHIGWIDDEN, Frank

7.1.1926 RUGLESS, Irene

26.1.1926 DUGAN, Thomas

19.4.1926 WILLIAMSON, Gertie Ruby

11.11.1926 WILLIAMSON, Hurtle A.

27.2.1928 PIERCE, Patrick J.

6.10.1935 LEE, John Keane

18.7.1939 LEE, Thomas Joseph

7.10.1940 EAMES, William Davis

5.5.1941 MATHOT, Jean Joseph

11.2.1946 THOMSON, Mrs Katie Symington

28.3.1951 KITTO, Keith Ernest

1.7.1967 MacKENZIE, Hugh Lloyd

2.10.1978 CIOT, Maurice Peter

8.6.1979 CIOT, Anne Marie

12.10.1979 CIOT, Maurice Peter

12.5.1980 WATERMAN, Raymond Peter

20.7.1984 FRANGIE, Anthony Dominic

26.6.1985 FRANGIE, Anthony Dominic

1.7.1985 FRANGIE, Anthony Dominic

5.8.1985 MELVIN, Stephen Jeffrey

7.11.1985 WATERMAN, Peter

10.3.1986 WATERMAN, Peter

20.6.1986 STURDY, Richard Gerald

14.5.1987 MANTO, Nicola

6.4.1988 MURPHY, Kevin Francis

22.7.1991 BENGER, Edward Robert James

7.8.1991 PISCITELLI, Edoardo

30.4.1992–93 – ? HANNAN, Thomas Wheldon

Norwood Hotel

97 The Parade (north east corner Osmond Terrace)

Norwood

Existed: 28.3.1850–1993 –? Rebuilt 1887

Known as Norwood Arms Inn 28.3.1850–2.6.1852

Known as Gold Diggers Arms Inn 3.6.1852–8.12.1884

Known unofficially as the Red Brick Inn Mid 1880s

Known as Norwood Hotel 9.12.1884–1993 – ?

28.3.1850 BROOKS, Abraham

3.4.1851 DREWERY, Isaac Curtis

3.6.1852 BRISTER, James

27.10.1853 JOHNSON, Henry

22.12.1858 MAYHEW, John

13.3.1871 WANSTALL, James

Mid 1876 LANDVOGT, J.P.

11.12.1876 WARNCKEN, Johann Anton

19.12.1884 MURPHY, Michael

7.7.1886 BOHM, Frederick William Albert

14.5.1897 CLARKE, Frederick

5.11.1898 PICKHAVER, Thomas jnr

20.6.1899 FINLAYSON, William H.

4.11.1899 PREWETT, Mrs Annie E.

10.8.1900 ABELL, Albert E. & McNAMARA, Patrick

24.10.1900 JACOB, William E.

4.1.1901 JACOB, Sophie

28.1.1901 CLARKE, Mrs Elizabeth W.

17.5.1901 AUSTIN, Frederick A.

19.8.1901 KENIHAN, John H.

1915 WATERMAN, Percy C.

1922 DALY, Jno. F.

1926 THOMPSON, Mrs G.V.

5.7.1927 TASKER, William Hampton

11.10.1943 TASKER, Mrs Albertina

3.9.1945 TASKER, Clyde Hampton

22.8.1951 OWENS, Horace Edward

3.10.1951 TASKER, Clyde Hampton

5.10.1951 OWENS, Horace Edward

16.11.1951 TASKER, Clyde Hampton

16.8.1953 OWENS, Horace Edward

20.9.1953 TASKER, Clyde Hampton

11.9.1955 OWENS, Horace Edward

21.10.1955 TASKER, Clyde Hampton

1.12.1965 TASKER, Clyde Hampton & Eveleen Maude

28.3.1970 HANN, Cecil George

8.12.1972 DEANE, James Grant

25.10.1974 DUNCAN, John David

28.1.1977 DEANE, James Grant

29.7.1977 OWENS, Wayne William

15.8.1977 SATURNO, Leon Edmund

16.5.1986 KING, Catherine Anne

10.10.1986–93 – ? SATURNO, Leon Edmund

Osmonds Hotel of Norwood

120 Magill Road (south side, west corner Osmond Terrace), Norwood

Existed: 8.3.1880–1993 – ?

8.3.1880	LEE, John Philip
2.2.1881	CREWES, Charles Frederick
11.4.1881	MELLOWSHIP, James
12.9.1882	CARLIER, Arthur William
10.2.1885	GOWENLOCK, Robert Thomas
11.9.1894	BLEECHMORE, Albert E.
27.8.1897	HUNTER, Ellen
11.12.1899	ROBERTSON, Joseph
18.1.1900	PORTER, Thomas
1905	WHITE, J.H.
1906	COTTERELL, W.
?–4.12.1906	COTTERELL, Mrs
5.12.1906	BINNIE, Robert
1910	RYAN, Mrs Alice
1917	WEBBER, Mrs M.E.
1922	PRATTEN, F.H
1924	BRANDON, Mrs. F.A.
1924	MADIGAN, T. R.
16.7.1925	CLANCEY, Mrs Mary
5.3.1971	CLANCEY, Joseph Ronald
21.12.1971	JAMES, Gregory Leighton
27.1.1972	BAILEY, Ronald Norman
11.2.1972	DUNCAN, John David
7.5.1973	HUNTER, Thomas Keith
21.5.1973	DUNCAN, John David
10.8.1973	HUNTER, Thomas Keith
5.8.1974	AULD, William Morton
17.1.1975	LONG, Desmond Lancelot Riggs
30.5.1975	SIMMONDS, Malcolm John
17.6.1975	DAVID, Helmut Max Walter
3.5.1979	RAPHAEL, Kevin John
21.7.1980	OPREAN, George
8.6.1982	JOHNSON, Peter John
18.2.1986	JAMES, Rosemary Patricia
1.7.1987	KEHOE, James Lyle
15.9.1988	DEGILIO, Bernhard Wayne
29.6.1990–93 – ?	HODGENS, Gregory Wayne

Prince Alfred Hotel

Norwood

Existed: 8.10.1863–Early 1864

8.10.1863–Early 1864	LEMMY, John

Rising Sun Inn

60 Bridge Street (east side, south of High Street), Kensington

Existed: 21.9.1848–1882

Known as Rising Sun Inn 21.9.1848–Mar. 1881 – ?

Known as Rising Sun Hotel ? – 13.12.1881–1882

Licence transferred (1882) to larger premises, the 'Rising Sun Hotel', a short distance away. These premises were refurbished and re-licensed in 1983.

21.9.1848	BECK, William
19.6.1851	INGHAM, Harry
1.4.1852	BECK, William
16.3.1854	BECK, Sarah Ann
26.3.1857	BECK, Mary Ann
24.2.1858	BECK, Sarah Ann
5.4.1866	BECK, William Alexander
9.4.1868	HAMBIDGE, John
28.9.1868	MOREY, Benjamin
10.6.1878	FAIRLEY, William Hamilton
8.9.1879	DUNK, John Palmer
Mid 1881	SMITH, Edwin Thomas
3.10.1881–Mid 1882	NEWLYN, Henry White

Rising Sun Hotel

Bridge Street (corner High Street), Kensington

Existed: 1882–1909. Licence lost following Local Option Poll.

1980s used as Flats. Licensed for one day (1982?) to celebrate centenary).

1882	NEWLYN, Henry White
10.3.1885	PAPPIN, Thomas Green
27.4.1887	FAULKINER, Thomas Percy
2.9.1887	GOTTSCHALK, Alexander William Julius
8.5.1888	CLARKE, George James
7.7.1888	ANDERSON, Mary Ann
23.9.1891	WOODING, Mrs Jane
28.3.1893	EVANS, Selina
18.9.1893	ROTHENBERG, Louis G.
13.11.1893	ROTHENBURG, Mrs Annie M.
18.12.1893	LEAHY, William
1896	LOGAN, James
23.2.1897	LAMBERT, William S.
12.6.1897	PEARSON, Thomas
18.8.1898	DEANE, Mrs Laura C.
Late 1898	LEWIS, William T.
10.5.1899	BYWATER, Benjamin W.
5.12.1899	KELLY, Mrs Eliza
19.6.1900	ROWE, James Thomas
10.4.1901	PFITZNER, Frederick W.
1903	WING, Richard
1904	GARIE, Mrs Clara
1906	FOODY, Jno.
1909	GEORGE, Walter J.

Robin Hood Hotel

315 Portrush Road [Kensington Terrace] (west side, south corner The Parade), Norwood

Existed: 19.3.1846–1993 – ? Rebuilt 1882

Known as Robin Hood Inn 19.3.1846–1872 – ?

Known as Robin Hood Hotel ? – 1876–1993 – ?

Possibly known as the 'Catherine Wheel'?

19.3.1846	BECK, William
1.4.1847	BOTTOMLEY, J.F.
Mid 1847	BECK, William
23.12.1847	TASKER, Thomas
Early 1849	Cessation of trading??
3.4.1851	TASKER, Thomas
31.3.1853	BELL, William
Mid 1853	JONES, David Thomas
22.12.1853	FAWCETT, Archibald
20.9.1855	THOMPSON, George
13.3.1856	DORNHEGGE, Casper Heinrich
13.6.1859	MART, William
15.12.1859	MacCARTY, John B.
27.9.1860	DEACON, Firmin
28.3.1861	NEWPORT, W.H.
3.4.1862	McLEAN, William
7.4.1864	BURMAN, Mortimer
14.12.1865	DUNCAN, George
10.1.1867	JENNINGS, John Hocking
8.6.1868	HENNING, Carl
2.9.1869	BRYANT, Mary
12.9.1870	BURMAN, Mortimer
12.12.1870	HAWKER, Thomas
11.3.1872	WICKLING, Ludwig F.
9.12.1872	WATERHOUSE, Charles Frederich
April 1876	WATERHOUSE, Mrs Amelia
23.8.1882	STONE, Francis Leonard
9.7.1889	DALY, Anthony
23.9.1889	WILLIAMS, Mrs Marianne
14.6.1898	PROVIS, Mrs Mary
21.8.1899	STOLTE, August
1903	STOLTE, Mrs Augusta
10.9.1908	PRESSLER, Fritz
1909	STOLTE, Mrs Augusta
8.9.1914	DAVIS, Mrs Anna Matilda
3.6.1957	DAVIS, Edward Joseph Bonner
1.11.1964	BRADY, Annie Doris & Christopher John
15.10.1972	McCAWLEY, James Edward
15.10.1977	LAWSON, Bryant & LAWSON, Mrs
31.10.1977	McCAWLEY, James Edward
31.3.1980	HOWELL, Peter Edward
23.9.1985	FLEMING, David
2.6.1986	THOMPSON, Michael Geoffrey
16.7.1986	HOWELL, Marilyn Denise
14.6.1988–93 – ?	CONOLLY, Susan Joy

Royal Hotel

2 North Terrace (south side, east corner Dequetteville Terrace), Kent Town

Existed: 10.12.1877–1993 – ?

10.12.1877	WILLIAMS, John
10.11.1881	GEORGE, George Lawson
30.8.1882	FENWICK, William Andrew
23.12.1882	FENWICK, Sarah Ann
5.6.1885	BLINMAN, Thomas
17.12.1888	TUCKER, Wallace
20.7.1889	GUDGE, John
10.11.1893	MEYER, Gustav
13.6.1900	JACOBY, Carl
1903	SHAND, Mrs Emily
3.4.1907	WILKINSON, Mrs Mary J.
1910	DeBUEHR, Mrs P.
1914	RICHARDS, Mrs A. P.
1919	MacDOUGAL, Mrs G.A.
1922	BADMAN, Mrs Mary A.
1924	BOND, Jno.
1925	HEFFERNAN, J.J. & M.
1927	HEFFERNAN, J.J.
1928	STONEHAM, H.C.W.
30.3.1931	SIGGINS, Mrs Rebecca Veronica
21.1.1946	BUCKLEY, Martin Joseph
16.12.1954	MADIGAN, Michael William
11.9.1955	STAINER, Howard Stanley Gordon
14.1.1957	WAYMAN, George Philip
22.2.1957	BARRATT, Richard Noel
26.8.1962	RINGER, George Arthur & Joyce Thelma
17.1.1966	CLARK, David John & Una Joan & TIDSWELL, James Lindsay Gottholdt
30.9.1968	BAROLO, Peter Victor
7.5.1969	PERRY, Harry Douglas
6.1.1970	CUMMINGS, Jasper Anthony
9.12.1971	CUMMINGS, Teresa Mary
12.6.1974	DULLER, Eugene Arthur
3.7.1974	CUMMINGS, Teresa Mary
25.8.1975	STANTON, Teresa Mary (formerly CUMMINGS)
2.10.1975	SANDERY, Allan Maurice
9.8.1976	DELLAPIA, Dominic & Eileen Regina
8.8.1979	SELTH, John Henry & SELPH, Margaret Joan
31.3.1982	TOMPKINS, Mark
24. 9.1982	AIKMAN, Geoffrey James
28.11.1982	PAECH, John Norman
17.12.1984	MacLEAN, Duncan Taylor
5.8.1991	GRANDIOSO, Nicholas John
10.2.1992	MARTIN, Nicholas Anthony
10.8.1992–93 – ?	TUNBRIDGE, Edward Robert Villiers

Vintage Shades

William Street (north side, east corner Elizabeth Street), Norwood

Existed: 29.6.1859–8.3.1909.

Known as Vintage Shades Inn 29.6.1859–Mar. 1880 – ?

Known as Vintage Shades Hotel ? – 1881–8.3.1909

29.6.1859	EDMUNDS, Joseph
17.4.1862	TOWNSEND, Jno.
2.4.1863	DOORNE, Henry
6.4.1865	JENNINGS, John Hocking
10.1.1867	ROBINSON, James
3.10.1867	LOGAN, William
8.6.1868	CLEARY, James
2.9.1869	BLAIR, James Jamieson
Late 1870	CLEARY, Catherine
12.6.1871	MAGAGHRAN, Patrick
8.9.1873	CLEARY,Mrs Catherine
May 1877	KEANE, Catherine
11.6.1877	KEANE, Michael
9.9.1878	MARTIN, Patrick
20.7.1880	MARTIN, Mrs Catherine
26.9.1882	CONRY, Bartholomew John
11.12.1894	CONRY, Mrs Hannah
10.3.1896	MURPHY, Margaret
8.9.1896	LAFFIN, James A.
9.3.1897–8.3.1909	RYAN, Mrs Alice

Index

Also published by the City of Norwood, Payneham and St Peters
in association with Wakefield Press

50 YEARS OF KENSINGTON AND NORWOOD 1853–1903

The City of Kensington and Norwood is one of the oldest inner urban areas of Adelaide. Early colonial descriptions picture a forest of gum trees penetrated by winding creeks full of wildlife and inhabited by the Kaurna people.

Within a decade, the villages of Kensington, Marryatville, Kent Town and Norwood were granted local government. By 1880, the Town of Kensington and Norwood was a major centre, with imposing civic buildings, theatres, institutes and sporting facilities.

50 Years of Kensington and Norwood provides unique insights into the settlement of this district. The reprinting of this book is an initiative of the City of Kensington and Norwood's Cultural Heritage Program.

ISBN 1 86254 420 4 RRP $12.50